SUCCESS
as a
FOSTER
PARENT

**Everything You Need to
Know about Foster Care**

D1015271

SUCCESS
as a
FOSTER
PARENT

Everything You Need to Know about Foster Care

National Foster Parent Association with
Rachel Greene Baldino, MSW, LCSW

ALPHA

A member of Penguin Group (USA) Inc.

CONTENTS

FOREWORD

I have been a foster parent for the past 32 years, and I served as president of the National Foster Parent Association (the organization that coauthored this book) from 1996 to 2000. In addition to having fostered many children over the years, my husband and I have two biological daughters and two adopted sons.

Simply put, foster parenting is my life's work, my calling. I feel so blessed to have worked with many wonderful foster children over the years. All of them have taught me so much and given me so much, and I will be forever grateful that these children and my family have been—and continue to be—such important parts of one another's lives.

Allow me to share some stories from my life as a foster parent: stories that I hope will inspire you and motivate you to pursue becoming a foster parent. My first story begins in 1993, the year my husband and I took in medically fragile twin girls. One weighed 1.6 pounds and the other weighed 1.8 pounds at birth.

The twins were so fragile that they spent the first year of their lives going back and forth between our home and the hospital. Both had feeding problems and shunts in the backs of their heads. One had difficulties with her shunt in addition to all of her other medical problems. We fostered these beautiful twin girls for three years, at which time the parental rights of their biological parents were terminated, and they became available for adoption.

During these three years, one of our adult daughters and her husband had been serving as the twins' respite foster parents to give my husband and me periodic breaks. My daughter and son-in-law did not have children of their own. Once the girls became available for adoption, we discussed the situation as a family. We also conferred with the Kentucky Cabinet for Health and Family Services—known to Kentucky foster parents simply as "the Cabinet." I am happy to report that the children were ultimately adopted by our daughter and son-in-law.

The twin girls, age 14 at the time of this writing, are now our beloved adopted granddaughters. They still have shunts in their heads and some other medical challenges, but, generally speaking, they are thriving, happy teenagers. I have to say, it's wonderful being their Grandma and Granddad. No discipline required, just love!

My second story takes place in 1975, the year my husband and I began fostering. Our own biological daughters were three and six at the time, and we were hoping to foster other small children. But the first call we received was a request to take in an 11-year-old girl who had run away from home. In a small-world twist, it was our nephew, a deputy sheriff in town, who had found the girl and brought her to the attention of the authorities. When this young girl first entered our home, she had not been to school for five weeks.

Ultimately, she stayed with us from the ages of 11 to 19, in a program once referred to as "permanent foster care." The parental rights of her biological parents were never terminated, which meant that she never became available for adoption. However, because of this permanent foster care arrangement, she was able to live with us rather than with her biological parents during her adolescent years. And did she ever thrive! For starters, she graduated from high school with honors. Eventually, with help and encouragement from us, she moved into her own apartment across the street from our home. Before moving into her apartment, she had worked for a full year at a McDonald's restaurant, saving half of her earnings to put toward future rent.

We were (and are) very proud of her. We admire her maturity, her strong work ethic, and her deep sense of responsibility. At the time, there was no formal name for what we did to help her get started as a young adult, with her first job and her first apartment. Nowadays, this process is officially referred to as finding an independent living situation for former foster teens—now young adults.

Later on, this young woman went to work in our dentist's office. Eventually, she met and married a young man who joined the Marines and they ended up in Hawaii. As I write these words, she is 43 years old and still living with her husband in Hawaii. He is now out of the service, but continues to work for the Marines in a civilian capacity.

During her time in foster care, we always made sure that she had regular visitations with her biological family. As I often say, "Children can never have too much love in their lives." And now, as an adult, she maintains—and cherishes—her strong ties with us and her biological family. Whenever she returns home to Kentucky, she stays with us. She also visits several members of her biological family. To this day, she is a lovely, thoughtful woman who always remembers everyone's birthdays and holidays and other special occasions. We treasure having her in our lives.

For my third story, I'd like to talk about a special day back in 1986 when we received a call to care for a medically fragile premature infant. He weighed three pounds and was on an apnea monitor because he was having breathing difficulties. We gladly took him in and he stayed in foster care with us for three years. He was then reunited with his mother, who happened to be pregnant with a little girl, although no one knew this at the time.

The biological mother allowed her brother to take the little boy for a while, but eventually she wanted him back. Arrangements were eventually made for the boy to live with his biological mother during the school year. He spent holidays and summers with us.

When he turned 15, however, things fell apart at his biological mother's home, and he had to return to our home on a more permanent basis. He was in high school at the time and was enrolled in special-education classes. However, after spending time with him, we became convinced that he did not belong in the special-education program. We requested that he be tested, and his test scores proved us right. Our educational advocacy on his behalf really paid off. After having been mistakenly enrolled in special-education classes all those years, he was moved into the regular classroom curriculum.

Around that same time, he entered the ROTC program. After graduating from high school, he went on to attend Mid-Continent University, a Christian liberal arts institution in Mayfield, Kentucky. He completed his course work and graduated in three and a half years, rather than the standard four. He is interested in studying to become a pastor, and in pursuit of that dream, he hopes to go to graduate school to earn his master's degree. This young man's younger sister, now age 14, lives with us. She has also entered the ROTC program, and she plans to follow in her brother's footsteps by going to college after she graduates from high school.

Now that I've shared a few of our many foster parenting success stories, I'd also like to offer some thoughts, observations, and suggestions about the foster care system in general. For example, one 14-year-old boy came to us from a neglectful home. While living with us, he did extremely well in school, earned excellent grades, and joined ROTC. He is now proudly serving his country as a Marine. When he comes home to Kentucky, he stays with us and visits with his biological family members.

Unfortunately, the Kentucky Cabinet for Health and Family Services terminated his biological parents' parental rights when this young man was just three months shy of his 18th birthday, because the Cabinet was in the process of terminating his parents' rights to his younger sister. While child welfare departments have the best interests of children in mind, they are composed of human beings, and human beings sometimes make mistakes. I believe that it simply did not make any sense for this young man to become available for adoption so close to his 18th birthday.

All of us—the young man, my husband, and I—objected vehemently, but the Cabinet ultimately chose to override our objections. This left him without any ties to a family, just as the state was going to release him from foster care, making him an orphan. What a transition—from the state caring for a youth 100 percent to the youth being released from custody with no family support.

As I mentioned, I have been a foster mother for 32 years, and I have seen the "policy pendulum" of departments of social services swing back and forth several times on a variety of issues. I can recall a time when foster parents were almost never encouraged to adopt foster children. Even in situations when adoption by the foster parents seemed like the best course of action for the children, the policy trend at the time dictated otherwise.

Today, the policy pendulum seems to have swung back in the opposite direction. In certain situations, such as when the biological parents' rights have been terminated, foster parents are now strongly encouraged to adopt the foster children in their care.

I would like to see more nuance in the system, a few more shades of gray, and a little less swinging of the policy pendulum from one extreme to the other. After all, the adoption of foster children by foster parents can be a wonderful option in many situations. But it is not always possible, nor always ideal. In cases when the child involved is a teenager—and therefore old enough to have a serious opinion on the matter—I firmly believe that the teenager's views should be taken into account during the decision-making process.

I'd also like to point out that permanent foster care, rather than adoption by the foster parents (or anyone else), can often be a viable—indeed a *wonderful*—option. This arrangement allows many children to have the best of both worlds: to live with stable, nurturing foster parents, while simultaneously having regular visits with their biological parents, who are also caring but perhaps less stable.

Another point bears mentioning: some foster parents are not interested in becoming adoptive parents. They feel a strong desire, perhaps even a calling, to serve their communities as foster parents, but they do not necessarily want to adopt. In my opinion, not only should their wishes be respected, but they should also feel free to advocate for this valid personal choice. Furthermore, foster parents who choose not to adopt should not be made to feel guilty by anyone inside or outside the foster care system.

As I mentioned earlier, I served as president of the National Foster Parent Association (NFPA) for four years, from 1996 to 2000. During my tenure as NFPA president, I worked out of my house, because the NFPA did not have an office at the time. I also happened to be caring for eight children in my home during that time. I was certainly busy and challenged, but I enjoyed every moment of it. As they say: if you want something to get done, give it to a busy person!

In 1997, as part of my job, I had the opportunity to visit the White House for the passage of the Adoption and Safe Families Act, and I met with President Bill Clinton and First Lady Hillary Clinton to discuss various issues and challenges facing foster parents. Both the president and the first lady took the time to learn about the needs and wishes of foster children and foster parents.

There are many things that I love about foster care and being a foster parent. One of my favorites is the fact that so many of the (now-grown) children we have cared for over the years stay in touch with us and choose to stay at our home whenever they return to Kentucky. I'm also happy that many of these now-grown children have good relationships with their biological families. After all, my husband and I worked hard—and continue to work hard—to keep the children's ties with their biological families strong and secure over the years.

My husband and I feel proud and honored to continue serving our community as foster parents, 32 years after taking in our first foster child. In fact, we feel as enthusiastic now as we have ever felt about opening up our home and our hearts to these wonderful children. They are blessings, every single one of them, and we feel happy and grateful to have had them in our lives, now and forever.

—Shirley Hedges, foster/adoptive parent and former NFPA president

INTRODUCTION

Foster homes fulfill an essential social need by providing for the physical health, emotional well-being, and daily care of children who, for various reasons, have been separated from their parents. If you are interested in becoming a foster parent, your initial explorations may leave you feeling that the process is very complex. But rest assured that every step is there to protect the welfare of children and to help potential foster parents understand and cope with their responsibilities. The system might not be perfect—what system is?—but over the years, many psychologists, social workers, child advocates, lawmakers, and other concerned professionals have put a great deal of consideration and effort into making foster care the best system for everyone involved.

Throughout much of recorded history it has been customary for extended family members—grandparents, aunts, uncles—to raise children who were orphaned or otherwise unable to remain with their mothers and fathers. There are several biblical references to this form of foster care. Old Testament law dictates that when a father dies, his brother should marry the widow to guarantee that the children would be raised with kin. Today, this type of care is referred to as kinship care.

In medieval Europe, some children who were orphaned or who had to leave home were raised in monasteries and convents where the monks and nuns served, in essence, as their foster parents. But after the Reformation, this custom fell out of practice. The English Poor Laws of 1501 mandated that townships provide care for their orphaned and abandoned children. Older children were apprenticed or placed in homes where they could learn a trade: perhaps farming or blacksmithing for the boys and domestic service for the girls. Infants, young children, and children with disabilities were usually kept at establishments known as "poor farms," where they received little in the way of education or supervision.

When the United States first became a sovereign nation, the English Poor Laws became the law of the land. Essentially, these laws placed impoverished children in indentured servitude until they reached adulthood. This situation was far from ideal; it allowed for the abuse and exploitation of countless children. However, during this same era, many people viewed the English Poor Laws as progressive, because indentured children were being taught valuable skills they could use later in life.

This legislation remained in place until the early 1800s, when a movement to place children in orphanages rather than in indentured servitude began. Unfortunately, orphanages were not an improvement over the Poor Laws. Many of the vulnerable, unprotected children placed in these institutions ended up suffering abuse, neglect, and mistreatment at the hands of the adults who had been designated to care for them.

In 1853, a critical year in the creation of what would ultimately become the foster care system in the United States, Charles Loring Brace, a New York City minister, founded the New York Children's Aid Society. Brace, who had grown increasingly alarmed about the high number of homeless immigrant children sleeping in the tenements and streets of New York, set up shelters and vocational training programs. He also established a system for providing these children with homes.

Brace believed that if he moved needy children out of the city and into rural areas, their odds of living a healthy, fulfilling, law-abiding life would vastly improve. He ran advertisements in newspapers in the southern and western states seeking families who might be willing to take in homeless children from New York City. Their reward, in addition to performing an act of charity, would implicitly be additional help around the house and farm.

One of Brace's biggest contributions to the new field of foster care was his creation of the orphan train movement. Through this revolutionary program, which was in place from 1853 to 1929, Brace and his colleagues placed more than 20,000 needy or orphaned New York City children in foster homes in 48 states. Unfortunately, in these early years of the foster care movement, some children found themselves in situations resembling the indentured servitude of the past. However, as flawed as the system was at the outset, the seeds had been planted for what would eventually become the modern foster care system.

The late nineteenth century brought additional milestones in the early foster care movement: In the early 1860s, Massachusetts started to pay board to families who agreed to care for children in need. In 1885, the state of Pennsylvania passed a law making it a misdemeanor to house two or more unrelated children in a home without a license from the state. And in 1893, South Dakota began to subsidize an organization called the Children's Home Society, which was founded to provide for homeless children in that state.

At the beginning of the twentieth century, the foster care movement began to take hold in American society. Agencies that supervised and provided training and support services to foster parents were established. Child welfare reformer Henry Dwight Chapin, a pediatrician from New York, founded the Speedwell Society, an organization that provided care for neglected and abandoned infants. Chapin disseminated fact sheets demonstrating that foster care was preferable to orphanages, in large part because so many children became sick and died in orphanage care.

Despite Chapin's and other child welfare reformers' efforts to publicize the many problems associated with orphanages, by 1910, there were still more than a thousand orphanages across the United States. Over time, however, opinion shifted in favor of foster care. In 1912, the United States Children's Bureau was created. Today, this agency falls under the auspices of the U.S. Department of Health and Human Services Administration for Children and Families. Currently, the organization's primary goals are the prevention of child abuse and the continual improvement of the foster care and adoption system.

In 1935, the Social Security Act built upon the efforts of the growing child welfare movement, providing services and programs for maternal and child health, disabled children, and homeless and neglected children.

By 1950, the number of children in foster care exceeded the number of children in orphanages for the first time in U.S. history. The tide was turning, and from this point onward, the foster care movement continued to gain strength and support. Foster parents began to be viewed as a significant part of an important team of professional adults working together to provide the best possible care for children in need.

In 1962, Ray E. Helfer and C. Henry Kempe published a pivotal work titled *The Battered Child.* This book introduced the general public to the ongoing plight of abused and neglected children. This book was then and is still considered an extremely important contribution to the child welfare movement.

The Child Abuse and Treatment Act (CAPTA), which became law in 1974, made it mandatory to report and investigate all credible allegations of child abuse. The law has been amended several times since it was first drafted, as more and more specific findings about child abuse and its prevention have come to light. This legislation provides federal funding to all 50 states to prevent child abuse, investigate and assess abuse allegations, and prosecute or treat those found guilty of child abuse.

In 1980, the passage of the Adoption Assistance and Child Welfare Act not only set aside funds for programs aimed at the prevention of child abuse, but also strongly promoted the reunification of foster children with their biological families. The term *permanency planning* was coined in the 1980s to describe efforts on the part of courts, foster families, birth families, social workers, foster care agencies, pediatricians, and other child and family advocates to establish plans for children to be returned to their birth families within a reasonable time frame when possible, and to pursue the next best options when this course was not feasible.

In 1997, President Bill Clinton signed the Adoption and Safe Families Act. This law, which had been championed by then–First Lady Hillary Clinton, lowered significantly the amount of time foster children could remain in foster care before becoming available for adoption. The Adoption and Safe Families Act was passed primarily to address the needs of those foster children for whom family reunification was not a safe or viable option. The law also strongly endorsed the oldest form of foster care, kinship care (and, when necessary, kinship adoption). These days, as soon as children are removed from their biological parents, child welfare workers begin investigating kinship care options, also known as *fictive kin* or *kin by custom*. The Adoption and Safe Families Act also offers generous financial incentives to states in order to encourage the adoption of foster children.

In 1999, the Foster Care Independence Act was passed, extending certain foster care services for young adults formerly in foster care from the age of 18 to the age of 21. This law acknowledges that young adults who have spent significant portions of their childhoods and adolescences in foster care have special needs. It increased federal funds to states in order to help youth transition successfully from foster care to independent, adult living.

The number of foster children in the United States passed the 100,000 mark for the first time in 1976, and the number has steadily increased. According to the American Academy of Child and Adolescent Psychiatry and many other sources, there are now more than 500,000 children in the U.S. foster care system. While it is unfortunate that so many children require foster care, it is gratifying that a national system is now in place to meet the needs of children and youth from disadvantaged circumstances. The system is far from flawless, and there will always be room for improvement and reform, but it must be said that, over the years, many nurturing foster parents have voluntarily stepped forward to devote their time, energy, and attention to children in need. Our nation owes them a huge debt of gratitude.

1

FOSTER CARING

In this chapter you'll find a brief overview of how the foster care system works, why children enter foster care, the basic criteria and legal requirements for becoming a foster parent, and the unique responsibilities and benefits of foster parenting.

WHO ARE FOSTER CHILDREN?

Typically, foster children have been removed from their biological parents (or other custodial adults) by governmental authorities. When officials determine that it is necessary to remove a child from his or her home, a county or state agency assumes responsibility for the care of that child and finds an appropriate foster home.

Children and teenagers may be taken by a state's or county's child welfare department and placed with a foster family due to the death, severe physical or mental illness, or incarceration of their biological parents. Children may also be taken from their parents if they have been deemed the victims of neglect or physical, sexual, or emotional abuse, or if their parents have been involved in substance abuse.

Children in the foster care system are of all ages and hail from all different cultural backgrounds, races, and religions. Many of them have brothers and sisters who also need foster care. Like children everywhere, foster children have their own individual likes, dislikes, abilities, and interests. Some have special needs due to physical or mental disabilities, medical fragility, language differences, or emotional or behavioral problems. (Sometimes these needs require specialized care and treatment in a facility, a group home, or the home of a specially trained foster family.) Some female teenagers may be pregnant when they are placed with a foster family.

Children remain in foster care until they can be safely returned to their biological parents or to a relative, or until the biological parents' parental rights are terminated and the child is adopted, either by the foster parents or by another suitable party. One or more staff members (often referred to as "caseworkers") from a foster care agency closely monitor a foster child's care in a foster home.

WHO ARE FOSTER PARENTS?

Foster parents are responsible adults who care strongly about helping children and teenagers and are willing to provide nurturing care in their own homes for displaced children and teenagers.

A foster parent serves as a certified or licensed "stand-in" parent, with the primary role of providing a child in need with a caring home environment and strong, nurturing, supportive supervision. Foster parents volunteer their time; they do not receive wages or a salary. They do receive a monthly reimbursement to cover the basic expenses of caring for foster children, such as food, clothing, and so on. The specific amount may be higher for children with special needs or medical issues. (As a rule, Medicaid covers the health-care costs of foster children.)

Some foster parents specialize in providing emergency care (usually for a month or less) until a more permanent arrangement can be established. Other foster parents prefer to provide long-term care for foster children who need more extensive attention.

BASIC CRITERIA FOR FOSTER PARENTS

To become a foster parent, you will have to meet some basic criteria. You must be a financially secure adult over the age of 21, and you must have a stable source of income. You can be a homeowner or a renter, and in many states you can be either married or single.

Having a stable existence of your own is, understandably, very important. But equally important is being the kind of person who always puts children's needs first. You must be willing to meet a child's day-to-day needs for food, shelter, clothing, nurturing, and medical attention. You must be ready to advocate for the children in your care in various settings, such as at school or in court. And you must be prepared to assist with implementing an appropriate "permanent care plan" for the child.

LEGAL REQUIREMENTS FOR FOSTER PARENTS

The foster care approval process varies from state to state. Generally speaking, however, you should be prepared to deal with a fair amount of paperwork and also be ready to submit your home and your household members to some degree of scrutiny.

A foster child's caseworker will have information about the exact approval process in your particular city, county, and state. Typically, though, you should be ready to …

- Apply for and obtain a family home license.
- Undergo a thorough background check (including a criminal history check).
- Have all the adult members of the household fingerprinted.
- Undergo a home inspection.
- Participate in a personal interview.
- Provide character references.
- Document your financial stability.

Many states also require applicants to undergo special training programs before qualifying as foster parents. If that's the case in your home state, successful completion of the training will be a prerequisite for licensing. If your state requires training, you'll have to commit to attending the training sessions and do whatever is necessary to complete the course.

THE ROLE OF FAMILY MEMBERS

Foster parents can be relatives or nonrelatives. When children are placed with relatives, this is called kinship care. Kinship placement and, when necessary, kinship adoption helps children maintain continuity with their extended families, their family histories, and their cultures. One of the benefits of kinship care is that it can offer children a new, safer home environment with the least amount of traumatic change. In addition, kinship foster care enables children to easily maintain contact with their birth parents when the court and the child's caseworker have deemed such contact safe and appropriate. Caseworkers, judges, lawyers, and other child welfare advocates should also bear in mind that many people, including those from Hispanic, Native American, and African American backgrounds, view forms of kinship care as a vital component of perpetuating their cultural heritage.

Recent studies show that many children fare better when placed with relatives than in foster care. And when children are initially taken from their biological parents, caseworkers first pursue placement with a family member. This should not, however, dissuade or discourage you as a prospective nonrelated foster parent. After all, when kinship care is not an option for a particular child, placement with a caring nonrelated foster family is almost always the best possible alternative.

A FOSTER PARENT'S UNIQUE RESPONSIBILITIES

Many of your responsibilities as a foster parent will be similar to those of all parents. All responsible parents seek to provide the children in their care with their basic needs, such as shelter, nutritious food, comfortable and weather-appropriate clothing, quiet sleeping arrangements, and protection from physical and emotional harm. They are responsible for their children's medical, dental, and mental health needs. They provide nurturing guidance as well as gentle, consistent discipline. Last but not least, they try to help their children grow and develop by exposing them to interesting and intellectually stimulating educational, cultural, and social experiences.

However, some important differences make foster parenting uniquely challenging. The differences between parenting one's own children and being a foster parent are significant, and it is important that you consider those differences before you commit to fostering a child.

EASING THE PAIN OF SEPARATION

Most foster children enter foster parents' lives in a state of anxiety and active bereavement over the loss of their family, home, neighborhood, and friends. This can be the case even if they were abused or neglected. No matter how hard their lives at home may have been, they will still miss their biological parents and everything that was familiar in their lives. It is human nature to prefer the known to the unknown.

A big part of your job is to help ease the inevitable pain associated with this separation. You will have to be sensitive to the child's feelings of disconnection and disorientation without trying to rush his or her adaptation. Understand that the child's mourning is bound to go on for a while regardless of how badly you want to end his or her—and your own—feelings of discomfort. Don't take it personally; know that it is part of an unfolding dynamic.

MANAGING "ACTING OUT" BEHAVIORS

Many children are in foster care at least in part because they have been disciplined too harshly in the past. For this reason, foster parents must take great care to discipline foster children firmly but *gently*.

In addition, children who are new to your household may withdraw or "act out" in order to test your boundaries as well as your patience. So another part of your job is to help them learn how to manage their behavior. You can help foster children learn to control their behavior by setting household rules—and consequences for breaking those rules—that are fair, consistent, and logical.

"Acting out" frequently takes the form of aggressive behavior or disrespectful talk. Teaching foster children to address everyone they encounter with a respectful tone and manner will serve them well during their stay with you and when they leave your home.

COMMUNICATING WITH BIOLOGICAL PARENTS

Foster parents are often asked to encourage an ongoing relationship between a foster child and the child's biological parents. You may even play a role in the actual visitations with the biological family.

Of course, in certain situations, foster children are not allowed to have contact with their biological parents. The foster child's caseworker will keep you informed about such matters. In situations where children are prohibited from having any contact at all with their biological parents, neither you nor the caseworker will arrange family meetings. In such cases, the protection of the children is paramount.

REWARDS OF FOSTER PARENTING

Foster parenting is a profoundly collaborative experience. When you become a foster parent, you become part of a critical-care team that includes the foster child's caseworker, doctor, legal representative, judge, other service providers, and, whenever possible, biological parents.

As a foster parent, you will meet a network of like-minded new friends, including other foster parents and those who support and believe in foster care. In short, foster parenting connects you to your community in a way that few other jobs or volunteer activities can.

Foster parents have an enormous sense of personal and professional satisfaction in knowing that they have played a critical role in helping children in need move toward safer, happier lives. Moreover, many foster parents find that the experience of caring for foster children takes them on a profound journey of self-discovery. You may learn that you have more patience and compassion than you ever imagined.

Foster parenting is a crucial job in our society. There is a continual need for it because literally thousands of children need foster care at any time. If you decide to become a foster parent, you will help these children feel cared for, supported, and safe by providing them with temporary or transitional positive parenting. In some circumstances you will also give biological parents enough time to get their lives back on track—and even though it will be hard to say good-bye, you'll have the satisfaction of knowing that you helped restore a family to wholeness.

It's enormously satisfying to help children in need feel genuinely secure and cared for, sometimes for the first time in their lives. Despite any challenges you may encounter, you will know you have made their worlds a better place.

KEY CHAPTER CONCEPTS

- The foster care system, which serves children of all ages and from all backgrounds, provides temporary care for children in need. Children are taken into state custody and placed in licensed, certified foster homes for a variety of reasons, including the death or illness of birth parents, parental incarceration, abuse or neglect, or parental substance abuse.

- Foster parents must be financially stable, responsible adults over the age of 21. In most states, they can be married or single, homeowners or renters. Foster parents are willing to put the needs of children first, to work collaboratively with other care team members, and to advocate on behalf of the children placed in their care.

- Legal requirements for becoming a foster parent include applying for and being granted a family home license; undergoing a background check, fingerprinting, a home inspection, and a personal interview; obtaining character references; and providing proof of financial stability. In some states, successful completion of preservice training is required prior to licensure.

- Kinship care refers to placing a child with a family member, rather than with a nonrelated foster family. Usually, caseworkers try to place a child with a family member first. If a kinship placement is not possible, caseworkers pursue other appropriate foster care options.

- The unique responsibilities of foster parents include helping grieving foster children cope with their feelings of loss after being separated from their birth parents and teaching emotionally struggling children how to better manage their "acting out" behaviors.

- The benefits of fostering include working as a team player with other dedicated professionals, such as caseworkers, therapists, doctors, and teachers, and becoming part of an active, thriving network of like-minded fellow foster parents. But the greatest benefit is the knowledge that you are making a genuine, lasting difference in the lives of children who need your nurturing care.

2

IS BECOMING A FOSTER PARENT RIGHT FOR ME?

Deciding to become a foster parent requires a great deal of forethought and soul-searching. No one should enter into foster parenting lightly; in a very real sense, children's lives are at stake.

This chapter guides you step-by-step through the process of deciding to become a foster parent, so you will know exactly which questions to ask yourself, and why. We'll talk about what it takes, in terms of character and motivation, to be an effective foster parent. We'll discuss how best to prepare your family for fostering when you decide it may be right for you. We'll also hear some words of advice from an experienced foster mother.

PERSONAL CHARACTERISTICS OF SUCCESSFUL FOSTER PARENTS

Foster parents need a few key personal qualities to provide foster children with the best possible care. First and foremost, you should be doing it for the right reason: a strong desire to help children. People who become foster parents for any other reason tend to burn out or lose interest quickly. Particularly, those who consider becoming foster parents for financial reasons will ultimately be disappointed, because the monthly reimbursement is usually insufficient to cover a foster child's living expenses.

As the last chapter noted, it is important to be a team player. A foster child's care team may include some or all of the following: the biological parents, other relatives, a caseworker, doctors, lawyers, and judges. The most successful foster parents are excellent collaborators who understand that no one can undertake a difficult job like foster parenting alone.

In addition to proper motivation and team spirit, foster parents need many other qualities.

BE ORGANIZED BUT NOT A "PERFECTIONIST"

Clearly, it's useful for a foster parent to be organized and responsible. You must be accustomed to having a busy—you might even say "jam-packed"—schedule and take pride in keeping appointments and arriving on time for planned events.

However, as much as it helps to be organized and conscientious, foster parents should not be perfectionists. They should not set unrealistically high expectations for themselves, their families, or any of the foster children in their care. This will only lead to frustration on everyone's part.

Eschewing perfectionism is also important when it comes to home visits. Foster care caseworkers will follow up on the children they place with home visits of varying frequency. Primarily they will want to see how you are managing and make sure you have a strong social support network in place, including fellow foster parents. It's important that you be comfortable with these home visits—and understand that it's acceptable for your home to look "lived-in" rather than spotless. Having a few dishes in the sink is not an indication that your parenting is flawed. On the contrary: children value your time and attention over a "spic-and-span" kitchen.

COPING WITH CHALLENGING BEHAVIOR

Many foster children, given their extremely challenging life circumstances, inevitably have difficult days when they struggle with depression, moodiness, and behavioral issues. They may act out, melt down, and say or do inappropriate things.

Foster children need foster parents who will understand their needs and not give up on them when they misbehave. Caregivers must be there for them emotionally, not only during their good moments, but also during their challenging ones. You need to be able to distinguish the child from the child's behavior. All "good" children have "bad" moments!

Patience and compassion are more than desirable virtues where foster children are concerned; they are absolute necessities. Helping children who have been abused or neglected to develop better behavior is a gradual process. No matter how badly you wish for it, it won't happen overnight.

Most foster children who have been mistreated will not be able to make the shift to appropriate behavior right away, so it's imperative that you give foster children the time and opportunity to get acclimated to your household while they work on improving their behavior. This doesn't mean "anything goes"; you just have to deal with their behavior fairly, firmly, and with understanding.

Remember also to praise children who make progress in controlling acting out behaviors. Reinforcing positive behavior is a good way to get it to "stick."

ASKING QUESTIONS

Foster parents shouldn't hesitate to ask questions about a particular child's history, health issues, emotional needs, possible length of stay, and the like. As the saying goes, "knowledge is power." The more you know about the foster children in your care, the better equipped you will be to help them.

Staying informed about a foster child's particular needs and goals means keeping open lines of communication with every member of the child's care team. A child's caseworker and other team members may be able to offer you valuable guidance and advice at crucial moments.

There are no silly or pointless questions when it comes to giving foster children the best possible care. If you don't know, ask.

CHAMPIONING THE CHILD

Another dimension of the foster parent's role is child advocacy. You may find yourself functioning as a foster child's spokesperson or advocate at school, in a courtroom, or with a caseworker, pediatrician, or the child's biological family member.

There are many circumstances in which you may be called upon to lobby on behalf of foster children and defend their rights. It helps if you have a strong sense of justice and aren't intimidated by authority.

MAINTAINING CONFIDENTIALITY

Children in state care have often been seen by a number of doctors, social workers, and therapists, and these care team members abide by a strict code of confidentiality as part of their professional ethics. Foster parents are asked to abide by the same rules when it comes to protecting foster children's confidentiality. It is of the utmost importance for foster parents to be discreet about all aspects (including psychological, medical, emotional, and educational) of a foster child's care.

In practical terms, this means not disclosing any confidential details of foster children's care and treatment to friends, family members, acquaintances, or colleagues under any circumstances.

GATHERING SUPPORT

Although it's important to keep the specifics of foster children's lives and treatment confidential, a foster parent can certainly talk to family members and friends about the general joys and challenges of foster-parenting. In fact, this is strongly suggested.

After all, as any psychologist or social worker will tell you, one of the best ways to alleviate stress is to talk about your feelings to a trusted confidant. So make sure that you have family members and friends you can turn to when you are feeling stressed out by the more challenging aspects of foster parenting. Your fellow foster parents can also be a particularly useful resource for information, support, and understanding, as can the members of a foster child's care team.

ACCEPTING FEEDBACK

When someone decides to become a foster parent, he or she must be prepared for a wide range of reactions from family members, friends, colleagues, neighbors, and others. Some may see potential foster parents as selfless saints; others may see them as getting in over their heads or "asking for trouble."

You may certainly listen to what those who care about you have to say about your decision to become a foster parent. At the same time, remember that becoming a foster parent is *your* choice (and, if you have a partner or other children, their choice as well). Ultimately, only you (or your partner and children) can decide what course of action is right for your immediate family.

SPOTTING A MISMATCH

Successful foster parents don't set superhuman expectations for themselves. Sometimes foster placements don't work out, and foster parents shouldn't panic if they feel mismatched with a particular child and have to request a change. If a particular placement is simply too challenging, make arrangements with the child's caseworker for the safe, peaceful removal of the child from your home.

Foster parenting is most effective between parents and children who work well together. If things don't work out the first time, it doesn't mean that you can't try again.

BEING ABLE TO LET GO

Understandably, foster parents become attached to the children in their care. It's hard to say good-bye to children who have lived in your home, befriended your own children, and learned new behaviors and coping skills while living with your family. However, in the same way that your own children must someday grow up and leave the nest, the foster children you care for must also take the lessons they have learned from you and incorporate them into the next chapters of their lives.

Will you be able to let go when the time comes? If you do the necessary soul searching *before* you become a foster parent, you may be able to determine whether or not you can emotionally cope with the fact that, in most circumstances, the foster children in your care will eventually move on.

Many experienced foster parents describe themselves as "professional parents" whose primary job is to provide a safe, peaceful living environment for children in need. If you view yourself as a "professional" with an important "job" to do, you may be able to avoid becoming overly attached to the foster children who eventually must leave your home.

However, it helps for prospective foster parents to know in advance that there can be a "forever" aspect of being a foster parent. Foster children frequently stay in regular contact with their former foster parents for the rest of their lives. Additionally, there *may* be another way you will stay connected: In some cases the foster care agency asks the foster family to become the child's adoptive family. Of course, there is no guarantee that this will happen.

Today most foster care agencies are required to engage in **concurrent planning,** which involves working toward a primary permanency plan for the child (such as reunification with the biological parents), while simultaneously working on other possible permanency plans (such as adoption of the child by the foster family), in case the primary permanency plan does not work out.

PREPARING YOUR FAMILY MEMBERS

If you can honestly say you are committed, motivated, patient, realistic, flexible, compassionate, nurturing, and up for a challenge, then foster parenting might be exactly the job for you. But in addition to being sure that you have the personal characteristics to be a successful foster parent, it is also important to prepare your family members for the possibility of becoming a foster family. Are *they* up for the challenge?

Caring for foster children can be particularly time consuming. It adds to your household chores (such as laundry, shopping, cooking, and chauffeuring). And if the foster children in your care have special needs, you must be prepared to invest a great deal of time in hands-on care, training programs, and multiple appointments with doctors and therapists. You will also need time to listen attentively to the foster children in your care, so that you can help them cope with their complex feelings regarding their biological families.

All of this can cut into the time a parent can spend with other family members. It's important to be certain that everyone is aware of the shared commitment you will all make and willing and able to make some sacrifices.

Any time you bring a new person into a family environment, every member of that family has to adjust to the shifting interpersonal dynamics. You and your entire family must make a strong commitment to fostering. In addition, the overall atmosphere in your home ought to be warm, relaxed, calm, and inviting, so that foster children sense immediately that they belong and are valued.

BEING "ON THE SAME PAGE"

In two-parent households, it is vital for both parents to "be on the same page" about becoming foster parents. It is essential to ask your partner if he or she is prepared for the changes that foster parenting will bring to your family life. This question will likely bring up many more questions, and you must be completely honest, both with yourselves and with each other, during these important conversations.

Your biological children will naturally be interacting with and sharing space, time, toys, and parental love and attention with the foster children who enter your lives. Are your children ready and able to do this? You may need to have several conversations with your children before you make your final decision about becoming a foster family.

BALANCING CAREER AND FOSTERING

Any working parent can tell you that balancing work and family takes the skill and focus of a master juggler. Foster parents who work outside of the home face unique challenges for a variety of reasons. Foster children have many appointments and meetings with doctors, caseworkers, school officials, and others at which a foster parent must be present. And some foster children and teenagers require constant supervision and behavioral monitoring.

The good news is that working people who want to become foster parents often find a variety of creative ways to balance a career while being a foster parent. As the saying goes, "where there's a will, there's a way."

A number of foster parents choose not to work outside of the home while they serve as foster parents. In a two-parent foster home, a variety of solutions are possible. One of the foster parents might work outside of the home while the other is a stay-at-home parent. Alternatively, one or both partners might switch from full-time to part-time employment. Still other parents might decide to work out of home-based offices. Some couples have one parent work at night while the other works a day shift, so that one parent is always home.

Before becoming foster parents, therefore, you and your partner should ask yourselves—and answer as honestly as you can: will we be able to give foster parenting our all if we are both working full-time outside of the home? If the answer is no, there's no harm in deferring your desire to foster to a later time and thinking meanwhile about how you might reshuffle your situation.

A FOSTER MOTHER SPEAKS

When it comes to deciding whether or not to become a foster parent, who better to advise you than someone with extensive foster parenting experience? With that in mind, we interviewed foster mother Bette Hoxie, who has successfully fostered many children. Here's what she had to say.

How did you make the decision to become a foster parent?

It was clear to my husband and me that we wanted more than three children, which was all we could have biologically, so foster care seemed like a place where we could put our love of family and children to use for a good purpose. We spent time with our three biological kids discussing how they felt about the idea. Our youngest had little to say as he was only a year old!

We were concerned about disrupting the children's places in the family, but they did not seem to mind. When we were asked to consider an older girl being placed with us, my oldest son simply said, "Well, she'll be the oldest girl and I'll be the oldest boy!" My daughter was as eager to share with a sister as she had always been with the two boys.

During your decision-making process, what were some specific questions you asked yourself, your spouse, and your children?

We considered how we would stretch ourselves to incorporate more of everything: food, clothing, household space, utilities, and extracurricular activities such as Scouts, church youth groups, music lessons, dance lessons, swimming, and all the various things we enjoyed at the time as a family. We also needed to invest in a larger vehicle.

Whom did you consult with during your decision-making process?

We knew no one who had gone through the process at that time. I did speak with my parents, who were aghast to think I would want to parent someone else's children. They came around, but it required work on our part to convince them that their grandchildren would not be lost in the shuffle.

Were your conversations with caseworkers or other agency representatives a factor in your decision?

The person we met with originally was a foster home certifier, also known as a licensing worker. She seemed confident that we were doing the right thing. After the first child was placed with us, we decided to make a geographic move. We wanted her to move with us, and that required some special interventions, but ultimately it was agreed upon that she would stay with us.

What feelings did you experience during the decision-making process?

I had moments when I wondered how it would all work out. But I was confident that the decision was coming from God and not myself, so I knew that it was the right thing to do.

What are some specific suggestions you have for people who are trying to decide if they want to become foster parents?

Think of adding a child as a new form of employment and consider thoroughly the implications of multiple meetings per week and other such things related to the work.

Should you think of foster children as still a part of their biological family or as part of your family?

Once you have the professional parenting or "employment piece" decided, think about what you have to offer a child and the child's family. Consider the child a part of a separate family until you have reason to believe the child will not be reunified with his or her own family. All the while during a foster care placement you are working towards reunification. Love the child as you would a biological child. That mind-set will help you to be more supportive of the biological family, and it increases the potential for successful reunification.

Simultaneously, though, begin to think about how this child will fit into your family for the rest of your lives. Children need people willing and able to commit for a lifetime, whether they are to be adopted by the foster family or not.

Are you supportive of lifelong connections between foster parents and foster children?

Lifelong connections are so important to healthy development.

Do you have any additional thoughts you would like to share?

Be absolutely sure, if it is a two-parent household, that both of the parents are in total agreement about moving forward to foster a child.

This foster parent's responses are instructive in many ways. She emphasizes that potential foster parents should have the proper motivation and that they should make sure everyone in the household understands the ramifications of foster care. Though she received some negative feedback from extended family members, she was able to go ahead with what she and her husband and children decided was the right course of action. In addition, she was able to accomplish the challenging emotional task of being willing to let her foster children go while at the same time embracing them as though they were permanent members of her family.

KEY CHAPTER CONCEPTS

- The decision to become a foster parent requires soul-searching to see if you have what it takes.

- Personal characteristics that many successful foster parents share include having the right motivation, being a willing collaborator, having patience with challenging behaviors and compassion for children who exhibit them, maintaining a professional attitude, and having the ability to "let go" when the time comes.

- It is imperative to make sure that everyone in the household—including one's spouse and other children—understands the ramifications of adding a foster child to the family mix. There will be more chores and more demands for parental attention. Be sure everyone can handle it.

- Foster parents who work outside the home face challenges in time management and in arranging for proper child supervision. If you and your partner both work, be prepared to implement creative solutions.

3

WHERE DO I START?

After you have carefully thought it over and decided that you do indeed want to become a foster parent, how do you get started? How do you find the right foster care agency for you? How do you begin the application and certification process? What interview questions will you be asked, and what answers are foster home certifiers seeking? What are foster home certifiers looking for when they inspect your home and property?

This chapter provides a road map through this research and assessment process.

BEGINNING YOUR RESEARCH

If you are thinking of exploring foster parenting options, the best place to start is in your own backyard, that is, with local resources. When staff at the National Foster Parent Association (NFPA) receive requests for information, they often direct prospective foster parents to their state foster parent association or state (or county) Department of Social Services.

There are two very practical reasons why the NFPA makes this recommendation. First, while several of the basic requirements for becoming a foster parent are consistent from state to state and county to county, there is enough variability among regulations to necessitate your finding out the specific requirements in your particular area. Second, since you will ultimately be working with your state foster parent association and your local foster parenting agency, it is helpful to familiarize yourself with their specific regulations, application requirements, and staff members as early as possible in your journey.

Generally speaking, you can find the contact information for these agencies in your local white pages (or sometimes yellow pages) or by conducting a methodical online search. The Internet can be a valuable tool for doing preparatory research before you apply to become a foster parent. If you enter the name of your state along with the phrase "foster parent association" or "foster care agencies" into a search engine, you will find a treasure trove of information.

Here's a great way to jump-start your research process. You will find a map of the United States on the NFPA website, www.nfpaonline.org. Click on your state to see contact information for your state's foster parent association. If you contact that association, a representative will give you the names of reputable, reliable foster care agencies in your community.

MAKING CONTACT WITH A FOSTER CARE AGENCY

When you make the initial phone call to your local foster care agency, you can expect the staff person to tell you about the basic requirements of foster parenting. You will receive a lot of useful counsel, but don't let the agency staff person do all the talking. It is also important to ask questions during this phone call.

If you have specific questions about your eligibility as a foster parent, this is the time to pose them. You will also want to know when and where the next orientation session for new foster parents will be held in your area. Finally, you should ask for the names and contact information of one or two experienced foster families in your community who enjoy talking to new foster parents. Speaking with experienced foster parents is a key part of your orientation and learning process.

THE APPLICATION PROCESS AND BACKGROUND CHECK

As a first step, you will be required to complete an application to obtain a family home license to be a foster parent. You will need to submit proof that you are 21 years of age or older. There is some variation from state to state regarding the exact personal information you will have to provide, but you will no doubt have to provide your current name and any other names you have ever used, your address and contact information, and your social security number and driver's license number.

INFORMATION ON HOUSEHOLD MEMBERS

Your foster care agency will also need information on the other people who share your home. All adults in your household—including you—will be asked to provide details on marital status, occupation, current employment, working hours, and gross annual income. The agency will also inquire about each adult's level of education. Sometimes, for statistical purposes only, the application may include a space for the adults in the household to indicate their race or ethnic background.

You will likely be required to list the names and dates of birth of all of the children in your household, including your biological children, stepchildren, and adopted children. You will be asked if you or any other member of your household has ever been the subject of an investigation by your state's Department of Social Services and, if so, why. You must report if a child of yours has ever been placed with other care providers and provide an explanation.

The agency will want to know if you have adopted children or have been licensed to provide foster care or day care in the past. It may also be necessary to reveal whether you or any other members of your household have received mental health services.

EMPLOYMENT AND HOUSING HISTORY

The foster care agency will ask you for information about your employment status to ensure that you have a stable, steady source of income. They might ask you to provide names and contact information for all of your employers in the last three to five years. They want to verify that you are dependable and have held a job consistently. Retirees and people on disability are often eligible to foster, so explain your situation if one of these circumstances applies to you.

You may be asked to provide information about the military history (if any) of all adult household members, including the dates of service, branches served in, dates of entry and discharge, and the type of discharge (honorable, dishonorable, or any other category).

The agency may also ask you to list all of your home addresses from the last three to five years. They will ask if you own or rent your current home or apartment. (Both owners and renters are eligible to become foster parents.) They may also inquire whether you live in a single-family home, a multifamily home, Section 8 housing, public housing, or other subsidized housing.

CRIMINAL BACKGROUND CHECK

You will be required to submit to a criminal background check. Each member (related or unrelated) of your household over the age of 18 will have to be fingerprinted. One or more of the questions on the application will ask whether you or any other member of your household has ever been arrested or charged by the police or has ever been arraigned, indicted, or convicted of any criminal offense in any state.

The criminal background check is primarily concerned with major criminal acts, such as domestic violence or drug and alcohol abuse. If you have a parking violation, a jaywalking ticket, or an overdue library book in your background, don't despair. Agencies are less concerned about relatively trivial matters.

HEALTH ISSUES

You may also be asked whether you or your partner have any chronic physical or mental illnesses or conditions that could physically prevent you from caring for a child with challenging behaviors. You may be asked to provide documentation proving that you and all members of your household who are 18 or older are free from tuberculosis.

On a related note, you may be required to provide the names and contact information for all physicians currently treating you and any other members of your household or to have a medical form completed by your physician. In almost all states, all adult household members must complete a CPR, first aid, and blood-borne pathogens training course. This is a good idea for any parent!

CHARACTER REFERENCES

You will likely be asked to provide the names and contact information for three or four individuals who have known you for at least two to five years. These individuals should be able to describe your personality, your parenting style, and day-to-day life in your household.

It's wise to inform your chosen references that they will be hearing from the agency with requests for these references, which they can submit confidentially. Let them know what your plans are with regard to fostering and be sure they support your goal. It's always a good idea to select character references who are comfortable describing their positive relationship with you.

HOME CERTIFICATION

As a potential foster parent, you will be required to show representatives from the foster care agency that your family life is stable and that your home will offer a safe, secure environment for a foster child. This process is usually referred to as a home safety inspection, a family home study, or a home assessment. In most instances, you will be required to open your home for inspection to representatives from the foster care agency and sometimes to fire inspectors.

Please note that you don't need to have an immaculate, dust-free, and clutterless home where you can "eat off the floor." People with comfortable, appropriately clean, but also "lived-in" homes are not turned away as potential foster parents. Above all, your caseworker wants to spend time talking to you in the comfort of your own space in order to get the clearest possible sense of your personality and parenting style.

HOME-SAFETY ISSUES

Although home certifiers are asked to describe to agency colleagues or supervisors the general "livability" and comfort level of the home, including an evaluation of the furnishings and overall housekeeping, there are also a number of specific safety concerns.

For the home-safety aspect of your home inspection, certifiers will want to verify the number of rooms in your house, including the number of bedrooms. If your home has more than one floor, they will approve one or more of the floors for sleeping. They will also examine the bedrooms intended for children to see what kinds of beds are provided. You will need to prove that your home does not contain lead paint (that it is "lead safe"). If you have a basement, agency representatives will check to see if it is finished or not.

Home certifiers will also note whether your home is constructed of brick, wood, or some other material. If you and your family live in an apartment, the certifier will want to know how many apartments there are in the building and if there is an elevator.

Home certifiers will also inspect the outside of your property and be asked by the agency to describe any garages (detached or attached), sheds, barns, outdoor play equipment, porches, decks, hot tubs, pools, ponds or lakes, and gates or fences. If you have a swimming pool, pond, or other body of water on your property, you will have to demonstrate that they are safely maintained and properly fenced.

If you have any pets, you will need to prove that they are licensed, that their inoculations (such as their rabies shots) are up to date, and that the animals are well cared for. You will also be asked if your pets are well behaved around children. The interviewer or home certifier will closely observe your pets' behavior around people during the assessment process. Hopefully, Fido and Fluffy will be on-board with your plan and on their best behavior.

If you own one or more guns, you will have to inform the agency and attest that they are stored in a place that is securely locked and inaccessible to children. If there are any smokers in the home, you may be asked to state whether smoking is permitted inside or only outside of the home. As you may be aware, exposure to secondhand smoke is an increasing health concern.

TRANSPORTATION

Home certifiers will also want to know how many and what kinds of vehicles are owned and operated by adult household members. They will make sure that all vehicles are in good running condition and properly insured.

Home certifiers will want to see if any of these vehicles contain infant or toddler seats, and, if so, to verify that they are properly installed. Certifiers may also inquire about nearby forms of public transportation, such as buses or trains.

AGE-APPROPRIATE PREPARATIONS

When you are getting ready for the home assessment, it can be helpful to consider all of the age groups of children that you anticipate fostering. For instance, if you anticipate fostering infants and toddlers, you will need to have a crib.

However, you should also know that in most communities, most of the children in need of care tend to be older (school-age children or teenagers). Therefore, throughout the assessment and orientation process, it is important for you to keep an open mind about the possibility of fostering children and youth of all ages.

THE INTERVIEW PROCESS

You will likely be expected to participate in a personal interview. Among other things, you will be asked about your motives for becoming a foster parent and how you plan to provide for a foster child in terms of safety, security, nurturing, guidance, and attention.

GENERAL FOSTER CARE QUESTIONS

Interviewers may ask you to describe your experience caring for children, such as parenting, teaching, or working in a day-care facility or as a nanny or babysitter. You may have to indicate whether you are single, married, divorced, or widowed. You may be asked how long you have been thinking about fostering, and, if you have a partner, which of you raised the subject first. If you are already a parent, you may be asked to describe your strengths as a parent and those aspects of parenting that tend to be challenging for you. (Every parent has challenging moments, so be forthright.) You may be asked to describe your religious affiliation or spiritual beliefs, and the role these beliefs might play, if any, when you become a foster parent.

Your interviewer may want to know how you heard about the particular agency or program to which you submitted your application, and why you want to foster a child through this particular department. The interviewer may also inquire about any previous direct or indirect experiences you have had with foster care, with their agency or any other. (If you have a friend who has served as a foster parent, you could mention it in this context.)

You may be asked to describe your general view of the foster care system—including your perception of the challenges faced by birth parents, your ideas about long-term commitments, your desire and ability to be a team player, and your willingness to abide by the rules of the child welfare system.

Some interviewers may want to know whether you have any specialized training, particularly in the fields of medicine, nursing, psychology, or social work. They will also ask if you are willing to participate in both preliminary and ongoing training in foster parenting issues.

PREGNANCY HISTORY

If you are female, you may be asked about your pregnancy history. For instance, an interviewer may say: "Many people have difficulty conceiving or maintaining a pregnancy. Is this something that you have experienced?" If you answer yes, you may be asked follow-up questions such as "Have you taken any steps to alleviate these difficulties?" and "Do these issues play any role in your decision to foster a child?"

TRAUMA HISTORY

Many interviewers ask foster parenting candidates if they have ever experienced or witnessed trauma or abuse in their own lives. They are referring to child abuse, sexual abuse, or domestic violence. If you respond affirmatively to this question, the interviewer might ask you to explain the circumstances. The interviewer might then ask if your partner is aware of your history and if you underwent counseling or took other steps in the aftermath of the trauma. The interviewer may also want to know how you have handled the relationship with the abuser since the period of abuse.

Interviewers are not prying when they ask foster parent applicants about past abuse. Rather, they are trying to determine whether applicants who have endured abuse can put those experiences behind them. For this reason, foster home assessors listen very carefully to the way in which candidates answer questions about past abuse. This enables them to clearly understand how these applicants might interact with foster children in their care.

Throughout your interview process, particularly when it comes to difficult, emotionally challenging questions, remember that all children—and perhaps especially foster children—need healthy, positive role models, adults they can trust and look up to as a consistent source of support, safety, security, and guidance. As a foster parent, you have the precious opportunity to change a child's life for the better. With every question they ask, interviewers are trying to accurately assess whether you have what it takes to rise to such an important challenge.

ADVICE FROM AN EXPERIENCED FOSTER HOME CERTIFIER

To help summarize the application process and provide related advice, we conducted an interview with an experienced foster care home certifier. Judi K. Martin is a home certifier based in Marion County, Oregon.

What is the first step in the foster care process in your community?

In our county, the certifier is not the first person to meet the potential foster parents. The potential foster parents start by completing the initial training, which here is called "Foundations." This training consists of eight sessions that "tell it like it is," meaning that it gives applicants the truth about being a foster parent. They hear about the rewards and the possible heartache, and hopefully this training course prepares them for this difficult job.

Then, if they are still interested, they fill out paperwork describing themselves, their home life, and their family, as well as the basics, like criminal history, medical information, employer references, school references, and four personal references. By the time I get their file, all this paperwork has already been filled out, they have completed the training, and their criminal history forms have been evaluated.

I also get feedback from the trainer about how the applicants participated in the training sessions, and if there are any special areas of concern. Then, provided there are no red flags, I schedule a meeting with the potential foster parents at their home.

What are the specifics that a typical foster care professional asks about in a home interview?

At their home, we go over all the paperwork and I talk to them about matters such as their motivation for foster parenting, whether they enjoy parenting, and whether they have time to meet the emotional

31

needs of a vulnerable child as well as to schedule counseling appointments, visitations with biological parents, doctor appointments, and so on.

We talk about the parents' personal history—about how they were raised, whether or not they were abused, and about their current relationships with their families of origin. We discuss their approach to discipline. Also, we talk openly about how they will deal with issues of reunification should their foster children return to their biological parents.

What do you look for in the home environment?

What does their home look like: Do they have the physical space for another child or children? Does their home feel welcoming, safe, and happy?

What happens after the interview and home inspection?

We look at the potential foster parents' references. We want to know how other professionals see them, and what their friends and family say about them—and, where applicable, what they say about them as a family or a couple.

How do you advise people who are at the beginning of the application process?

I advise them to talk with other foster parents, maybe spend an evening in their home. I encourage them to take the initial training, because it is very good at helping people decide if they are ready for fosterparenting or not. I also encourage them to establish an ongoing relationship with current foster parents and possibly even do respite foster care—short-term, temporary care for families with extenuating circumstances—as a way to get started.

What are some "stumbling blocks" or challenges?

The most typical thing I see is people having difficulty with getting all the paperwork submitted in a timely fashion. The other is that if they have lived out of the state within the past five years, they need to be fingerprinted, and the fingerprints typically take 30 to 60 days to get back. We cannot place children until that is all back, so that takes some time.

Which specific resources and information do you think are the most valuable for all foster parents, but especially for new foster parents?

I think connecting with experienced foster parents is the most valuable. Many of our applicants already know another foster family, but if not, foster parents can be found at support groups—and hopefully at a support group that doesn't just sit around and grumble about things that can't be changed.

Also, here in Marion County, applicants get a lot of written material at the Foundations training.

What would you say to individuals who are considering becoming foster parents, and who believe they would do a good job, but feel anxious or intimidated by the approval process?

Get to know the system through people that are already in it. Then step out and try it for yourself. After talking to current foster parents, offer to do respite care.

Also, taking the preservice foster parent training cannot hurt. All it can do is give you more information and equip you better to make that big decision.

Do you have any additional thoughts, insights, or tips for people who are considering becoming foster parents, or who are just starting out as foster parents?

I would assure them that they can make a difference in a child's life. All you need is a willing heart, a willing family, and some time. In my opinion, some of the best foster parents are the ones who only take one child. They make that child feel like family.

COMPLETING THE ASSESSMENT PROCESS

The agency staff member who interviewed you and assessed your home will be asked to provide a written assessment of your potential foster parenting abilities to agency colleagues and supervisors. The interviewer may be asked to describe your general personality and personal history, with a particular focus on your level of empathy, your maturity and emotional stability, and your parenting skills, as well as your ability to manage stress and relate well to others. The interviewer may also be asked to describe your overall view of the foster care system and to state what is motivating you to become a foster parent.

When the assessors have determined that you meet all the criteria, and you have attended all mandatory preservice training sessions, you will receive a written statement informing you that you have been approved and are officially licensed to serve as a foster parent.

When there's an opportunity for your first placement, you will likely receive a phone call from a caseworker at the foster care agency telling you about a particular child who needs to be placed. You will be given some preliminary information about that child's specific situation and needs. Ask questions! See if it feels like an appropriate match for you.

If you go through the application process and are rejected, you should feel free to ask your interviewer or home assessor to tell you why you were turned down. Perhaps you can easily correct the problems, in which case, you might reapply. Bear in mind, however, that you will probably be required to indicate that you are applying for the second time and describe why you were rejected the first time. You will also have to spell out in detail what changes you have made to correct any problems.

If you're not willing or able to make the changes necessary for approval, you might decide not to reapply. The good news is that even if foster parenting turns out not to be the right choice for you, there are countless other ways to help children in need. For instance, you can volunteer to work with children through schools, Scouting, or through mentoring organizations like Big Brothers and Big Sisters. You can donate clothes, books, school supplies, toys, or funds to your local Boys' and Girls' Club or to other worthy children's charities.

FOSTER CARE BILLS OF RIGHTS

As you consider foster parenting and go through the application process, you might want to review these important and inspiring documents.

Sixteen states have enacted a bill of rights for foster parents. Each bill of rights is worded slightly differently, but they have many points in common. For instance, nearly all of them declare (in one way or another) that all foster parents have the right to be "treated with dignity, respect, trust, value, and consideration as a primary provider of foster care and a member of the professional team caring for foster children." (This particular quotation is from Alabama's Foster Parent Bill of Rights.)

Some states have taken this idea one step further, officially outlining not only a foster parent's rights, but also a foster parent's responsibilities. For instance, in 2001, the state of Washington, inspired by the Child Welfare League of America, and in collaboration with the state's Department of Social and Health Services and several foster parent "work groups," created an official statement of "Foster Parents' Rights and Responsibilities." You can find the statement on the department's official website, at: www.dshs.wa.gov/ca/fosterparents/be_FosterRights.asp.

Some of the responsibilities listed in this document include "the responsibility to respect a child's biological family, traditions, culture, and values" and "the responsibility to work cooperatively with agency staff as members of the child's team."

Regarding a foster parent's rights and responsibilities, another extremely helpful document you may want to review is the "Code of Ethics for Foster Parents," available on the NFPA website, www.nfpaonline.org.

Of course, just as foster parents have official rights, foster children have rights. Theirs are enumerated in a national bill of rights that applies to all foster children throughout the United States. The Foster Child Bill of Rights was ratified in 1973 and reaffirmed during the National Focus on Foster Care Conference in 1983. According to the Foster Child Bill of Rights, every child in foster care has the inherent right …

> *to be cherished by a family of his own, either his family helped by readily available services and supports to resume his care, or an adoptive family or, by plan, a continuing foster family.*

> *to be nurtured by foster parents who have been selected to meet his individual needs, and who are provided services and supports, including specialized education, so that they can grow in their ability to enable the child to reach his potentiality.*

to receive sensitive, continuing help in understanding and accepting the reasons for his own family's inability to take care of him, and in developing confidence in his own self worth.

to receive continuing loving care and respect as a unique human being … a child growing in trust in himself and others.

to grow up in freedom and dignity in a neighborhood of people who accept him with understanding, respect, and friendship.

to receive help in overcoming deprivation or whatever distortion in his emotional, physical, intellectual, social, and spiritual growth may have resulted from his early experiences.

to receive education, training, and career guidance to prepare for a useful and satisfying life.

to receive preparation for citizenship and parenthood through inter-action with foster parents and other adults who are consistent role models.

to be represented by an attorney-at-law in administrative or judicial proceedings with access to fair hearings and court review of decisions, so that his best interests are safeguarded.

to receive a high quality of child welfare services, including involve-ment of the natural parents and his own involvement in major deci-sions that affect his life.

For additional information about the Foster Child Bill of Rights, visit the NFPA website.

KEY CHAPTER CONCEPTS

- The initial research process for becoming a foster parent typically involves contacting your state or county Department of Social Services and your state or county foster parent association. If you wish to conduct your research online, the NFPA website, with its many links to state and local resources, is a great place to start.

- The application process includes filing paperwork detailing your and your family members' personal, health, educational, and employment histories. The application process also includes a criminal background check, fingerprinting, and the submission of character references.

- As part of the application process, your home will be inspected for livability and for safety.

- During the interview process, the topics you may be asked to discuss include all of your previous experiences with caring for children, your partner's views of fostering, your upbringing and your relationship with your family of origin, your strengths as a parent, and which aspects of parenting you find the most challenging.

- If your application is accepted, you will receive word in writing informing you that you are officially licensed to serve as a foster parent. If your application is rejected, you may reapply after correcting whatever problems were found.

4

TRAINING AND ONGOING SUPPORT FOR FOSTER PARENTS

It is important for foster parents to view themselves as "professional parents." One aspect of being a professional is participating in orientation and training. Indeed, in many states you will be required to participate in preservice training courses before becoming a certified foster parent. Moreover, once you've been certified, you will be expected to attend in-service training classes in specific areas of foster care. This chapter describes the various orientation, training, and support programs available to you as you navigate the foster care system.

ORIENTATION SESSIONS

A key part of your initial information-gathering process will be to attend a foster parent orientation session at your local social services office. To find out when the next orientation session will be held in your area, contact your state foster parent association or your local Department of Social Services, or visit your state foster parent association's website.

You obtain information specific to your state and county at the orientation session. However, in addition to these specifics, expect a question-and-answer session that includes the following general information.

Can you choose the age of a foster child?

In some instances, you can. You might want to foster children of different ages, however, before you decide to specialize in fostering a particular age group.

At the present time, the groups most in need of foster care are children between the ages of 11 and 16, sibling groups, and teenage mothers.

What is the length of a foster placement?

A foster placement lasts for as long as it takes to achieve a satisfactory, permanent placement for the child. The Adoption and Safe Families Act (1997) states that the goal of each foster placement is to find a permanent home for the child as quickly as possible.

There is no way to predict how long this may take at the beginning of a placement. However, according to Prevent Child Abuse America, as of 2001, approximately 20 percent of foster children remain in foster care for 5 months or fewer, while 45 percent remain for 18 months or fewer, and 35 percent stay for 3 years or longer.

Keep in mind that, as a foster parent, you can provide input in the development and implementation of each foster child's permanency plan. This is accomplished in collaboration with your licensing foster care agency, any other involved social services agencies, and often, depending upon the specifics of the case, with the child's biological parents.

Can single adults serve as foster parents?

In many circumstances, the answer is yes. However, some states do not license or certify homes for foster care if the adults living in the house are not married or related.

What are the age and financial requirements?

You must be 21 or older to be a foster parent, but there is no upper age limit. A high income is not required, but you must be financially stable and able to pay your monthly bills *without* reliance on foster care stipends. You can be either a homeowner or a renter, and, in some (though not all) cases, a foster child can share a room with another child of the same gender.

What are the training commitments?

In addition to your initial orientation session, you will probably be required to take part in several hours of preservice training. Ongoing training is also available in most states for foster parents who want to continue their parenting education and who are eager to stay well informed about the latest findings in foster care research and child development issues.

What kind of outside support can we expect?

Each foster child is assigned a caseworker who is familiar with the child's background and needs. You can turn to the caseworker for information and support on many levels. For example, the child's caseworker can answer questions you have about foster parenting in general, the particular child in your care, or any crisis that involves a foster child.

If you are feeling an excessive level of stress, remember that respite care is often available to provide you with a brief time out. During your orientation session, feel free to inquire about respite services for foster parents in your county and state. You can also turn to your local foster parent support group for advice and encouragement.

A number of foster care agencies offer crisis-level support and interventions to foster parents. For instance, some agencies provide their foster parents with a crisis hotline that can be called 24/7 in case of an emergency.

How are health-care issues handled?

It is the foster parent's responsibility to see that the foster child's medical needs are met. It is up to you to take foster children to all necessary appointments, to follow up with doctors, and to dispense medication as prescribed. In most states and localities, Medicaid covers most of the costs of foster children's health care.

What is the advocacy aspect of foster parenting?

Advocating for foster children might involve working with the school system to make sure that the children are receiving testing or special educational services as needed. You may also have to advocate for foster children in the courtroom to develop a permanency plan that is in their best interests. This often involves working collaboratively with the children's birth parents, caseworkers, and lawyers. Foster parent support groups often advocate for services.

How do I pay for the costs of caring for foster children?

Foster parents receive a monthly reimbursement to cover the cost of foster children's food and clothing. If you work outside of the home and the foster children in your charge will require day care (which must be agency approved), you are usually responsible for covering the cost.

Can foster children accompany foster parents on family vacations?

Generally speaking, they can, with permission from the children's caseworkers. Be sure to ask if permission is required for the children to cross county or state boundaries.

How should foster parents handle holidays and other get-togethers with extended family?

It's best if foster children know what to expect in such situations so they will not feel overwhelmed. Talk about family traditions and practice good manners with foster children before family and holiday get-togethers. Try to get foster children and your extended family members together at least once *before* a holiday—on a more relaxed occasion. Also, although holidays are typically times of talking and sharing, do keep in mind the importance of maintaining confidentiality about foster children's life situations.

What behavioral issues might foster parents encounter?

In some situations, foster children may withdraw from their foster parents. The reasons vary. Perhaps they are grieving the loss of their birth parents. If they have been victims of abuse or neglect, they might find it hard to trust adults or to believe that acts of kindness and nurturing are genuine.

At other times, foster children might deliberately try to anger or provoke you. Prevent Child Abuse America suggests that they might, on some level, be trying to recreate the world of angry adults with which they are familiar.

It's important to remember that none of these behaviors are an indictment of you. This lack of trust and these inappropriate behaviors are often habitual responses, emotional defense mechanisms, or coping methods that children have developed over time. In your preservice and in-service training sessions, you will learn more about the variety of challenging behaviors foster children may exhibit and how to be prepared to handle such situations in your own home.

Can foster parents adopt foster children?

Remember that in many instances the ultimate goal of foster care is to return the child to his or her biological parents. If this is not possible, and if kinship placements are also not possible, a foster child may be adopted by the foster parents, or by someone else.

Can "letting go" ever be a positive experience?

As difficult as letting go of foster children can be, it can also be a time of healthy emotional closure. It can be a "graduation" of sorts—the end of a critically important life chapter, for both you and the foster child.

PRESERVICE TRAINING

Foster care agencies do not expect to get fully formed foster parents right out of the box. As noted earlier, most states require potential foster parents to attend preservice training courses. Preservice course materials vary from state to state, but many of the same topics are covered.

A SAMPLE PRESERVICE CURRICULUM

Betsy Keefer Smalley is the program manager of the Adoption and Foster Care training components of the Ohio Child Welfare Training Program. In Ohio, the Institute for Human Services (IHS) provides 36 hours of high-quality, interactive preservice training prior to foster parent licensure. Classes are offered in the evening and on weekends to accommodate busy working adults.

Ms. Keefer Smalley provided us with an overview of the general curriculum of the IHS preservice training course (reprinted here with permission):

Orientation and Overview—This workshop provides an overview of the child welfare system and examines the differences between foster care, adoption, and kinship care. Participants receive information about the needs of waiting children as well as the process of becoming a caregiver.

Teambuilding—This workshop discusses the history of foster care/adoption and examines the role of the foster/adoptive/kinship caregiver within that system. Information is shared about the effective use of teams to serve children.

Abuse and Neglect—This workshop examines the dynamics of child maltreatment. The trainer also seeks to develop empathy for the birth parent or caregiver who has abused or neglected a child. Participants view a video about an abusive birth parent, and they view a set of slides which depicts the signs of child maltreatment.

Child Development—This workshop gives participants an overview of normal child development and examines the impact of abuse and neglect on child development.

Attachment and Separation—This workshop demonstrates normal, healthy attachment and the impact on attachment of separation from primary parents, siblings, and other attachment figures. Participants also learn methods to reduce the trauma to children who have experienced separations from significant others.

Discipline—This workshop examines the reasons for behavioral problems among foster and adopted children. The workshop also explains the agency policy regarding corporal punishment and the underlying reasons for that policy. Finally, participants receive information on positive ways to manage behavior including natural and logical consequences, contracting, and rewards.

Working with Primary Families—"Primary families" is another term for biological or birth families. This workshop provides information about the losses experienced by birth families, expected behaviors of grieving birth parents, and ways to work effectively with birth families along a continuum of contact. A birth parent speaks to the training group about his or her experiences with foster care.

Cultural Issues in Placement—This workshop presents an overview of culture and the ways in which our values and codes of conduct are impacted by culture. Participants learn to separate culture from race and learn to identify the many and complex ingredients of cultural identity. Caregivers will also learn methods to more successfully parent a child from a culture different from their own.

Caring for Children Who Have Been Sexually Abused—This workshop examines the definition and dynamics of sexual abuse of children. The workshop also helps prospective parents develop an awareness of the characteristics of caregivers that lead to success in parenting children who have been sexually abused.

Effects of Caregiving on the Family—This workshop examines the impact of foster care/adoption/kinship care on the family system. The workshop also enables prospective parents to develop effective coping strategies and survival plans.

Permanency Issues for Children—This workshop examines the effect of long-term separation from the birth family (either by adoption or long-term foster care) on children. The workshop will explain some triggers that may exacerbate difficulties of children experiencing these long-term separations.

Permanency Issues for Families—This workshop examines the impact of adoption issues for adoptive parents on the family system. The workshop also explores techniques of talking with the children about their adoptive status and difficult birth histories. Finally, information about post-adoption services is shared with prospective parents.

CHILD DEVELOPMENT

Learning about child development is a significant part of preservice foster parent training. Childhood is a time of immense psychological, social, cognitive, and physiological change. You wouldn't expect the same behaviors and the same level of understanding from a 3-year-old as from a 9-year-old or a 13-year-old. In order to parent appropriately, it is important to know the developmental milestones most children reach at certain ages.

When you have a thorough understanding of what is considered "typical" development at any given age, you have a better sense of the special needs of foster children in your care. You can help them apply skills, deal with their peers, and achieve a sense of accomplishment based on their strengths and capabilities.

Understanding child development milestones can also help foster parents spot indicators of possible developmental lag. If a behavior persists beyond the time it is expected, or if new, advanced behaviors do not arise, you can seek whatever advice and input you need.

Finally, understanding the normal characteristics of various age groups in physical, emotional, social, mental, and moral areas will help you develop effective parenting behaviors. A parent who has been trained to understand that appetite increases in adolescent males—and that rapid growth may also bring on a lack of energy—will have also been trained to refrain from nagging teenage boys about food intake and laziness.

"The Child Development Guide" is an extremely useful 86-page online manual published jointly by the New York State Office of Children and Family Services and the Center for Development of Human Services (CDHS) at SUNY/Buffalo State College. To access the guide, go to the CDHS website, www.bsc-cdhs.org, and click on the "Child Development Guide" link.

COMMUNICATION SKILLS

Communication, both verbal and nonverbal, is another important topic covered in many preservice training courses. Trainers may suggest verbal helping skills including ...

- Asking "open" or "open-ended" questions to invite a child to speak frankly about a wide range of topics.

- Asking "closed" or very specific questions to get highly focused answers from a child on a particular topic.

- Asking clarifying questions—who? what? when? where? how?—to resolve ambiguous communications from a child.

- Frequently checking in with foster children by asking them gentle, nonthreatening questions about how they feel or what they think about certain experiences and situations.

No training in communication would be complete without some mention of the importance of listening attentively. A trainer will help you find ways to indicate that you are listening actively, for example, by repeating or paraphrasing things the child has said or by "matching" your facial expression, tone of voice, and body language to mirror the emotions of the child.

Communications courses also focus on nonverbal communication, which can be as meaningful as words. One nonverbal helping skill for foster parents often described in preservice courses is creating a comfortable environment by removing physical barriers and minimizing outside distractions. Another is using encouraging body language, such as appropriate eye contact and supportive facial expressions, posture, and gestures, as well as a gentle, soothing tone of voice.

Many such preservice communications courses include information on the importance of reading with children. Reading aloud has been proven to provide measurable intellectual stimulation to even the youngest of children. Reading aloud to infants, for instance, helps them learn how to recognize and respond to the voices of their parents or primary caregivers. Reading together is also a wonderful way to bond.

MANAGING CASEWORKER VISITS

In your preservice training you will learn about ongoing home visits and how they are helpful to all parties: the child's caseworker, the foster parent, and the foster child. Home visits can serve different purposes. For instance, a foster child's caseworker may use a home visit to sit and observe how things operate in your household. During another home visit, the caseworker may want to talk directly with you or the foster child about how the child is coping, both at home and at school.

It can be helpful to think of home visits as valuable communication opportunities for you, the caseworker, and the child to discuss specific concerns. As well, periodic home visits give all of you the chance to assess a particular child's progress.

INTERACTING WITH BIRTH PARENTS

During your preservice training, you will hear a great deal about the role of birth parents in foster children's lives. As you know, the role of the child's birth parents will vary from case to case. In some instances, the birth parents may not be involved at all, whereas in other situations the birth parents may be fully engaged in the child's life. The child's caseworker will keep you informed about the birth parents' level of involvement in your particular situation, including how to arrange and coordinate visits with the child's birth family if that is part of the treatment plan for a particular family.

IN-SERVICE TRAINING

In addition to orientation and preservice sessions, you will have many opportunities to *continue* training as a foster parent. Your state foster parent association may, for instance, sponsor one- or two-day seminars on a specific topic of interest to foster parents. Fellow members of your local foster parent support group can be a good source of information about upcoming training events. Keep yourself tapped into local and national foster parenting networks. Check the NFPA website regularly in order to find out when training conferences, seminars, workshops, events, and courses are being offered.

The required number of in-service training hours varies significantly from state to state. The caseworkers at your agency or representatives from your state foster parent association will tell you how many hours of in-service training you will need per year.

SPECIALIZED CLASSES

In some cases you may have the option to attend workshops on specific topics that are of special interest or concern to you. Such topics may include …

- Parenting from a "strengths perspective."
- The importance of play in childhood.
- How to work with behaviorally challenged children.

- How to care for children with Attention Deficit Hyperactivity Disorder (ADHD).

- How to help children who wet the bed.

- How to communicate effectively with a foster child's biological family.

- How to address attachment or bonding problems in children.

- How to care for children with developmental disabilities.

In-service training is also available online from companies such as Foster Parent College (part of the SocialLearning.com website) and Fosterparenttraining.com. Online in-service training can be a convenient option, particularly for foster parents with busy schedules. One caveat: Make sure that the online training institute you choose is reputable and that their courses are accepted as a valid form of training in your state. Despite its convenience, one drawback of online training is that you miss out on the opportunity to talk and network with your fellow foster parents.

However you train, always hang on to documentation (such as certificates of completion) showing that you have fulfilled a requirement or completed a particular in-service course, because you may be required to produce this evidence later.

ADVOCACY TRAINING

Another form of training offered to foster parents is in-service advocacy training. Advocacy can be somewhat intimidating for new foster parents. Many new foster parents, however, may already be functioning in the role of advocate for their foster children and not even realize it! Essentially, every time you stick up for a foster child's rights in school, at the courthouse, or in any other setting, you are functioning as an advocate.

Foster children need strong advocates at school for many reasons. According to the NFPA, "children and youth who are or have been in out-of-home care face extra challenges: more than 60 percent of children or youth in care drop out of school before graduation, a rate that is twice as high as the dropout rate for all students." In addition, children and youth who are or have been in out-of-home care are two or three times more likely than other students to have disabilities that affect their ability to learn.

For more detailed information about advocating for foster children, visit this page on the NFPA website, NFPAonline.org. The page offers a basic online training course called "Advocacy 101," as well as a slide presentation about the many benefits of advocacy. It also addresses the importance of advocating for foster children at school.

According to the same NFPA report, there are many reasons why some foster children do not fare well in school. Many foster children have been subjected to one or more serious traumas, such as abuse, violence, neglect, abandonment, and separation from their birth families. They may also experience substantial gaps in their educational experiences. Due to transitioning from one home to the next or for other reasons, they may have fallen behind in their schoolwork, or they may not have attended school consistently prior to placement in foster care.

Many children in foster care also face language barriers, medical problems, or behavioral issues and challenges that can further impede their progress in school. A lack of communication among some or all of the child's care team members can also disrupt a foster child's educational experience.

Ultimately, advocacy training will show how serving as an educational advocate for foster children comes down to checking in daily with the children themselves. Ask them directly about how they perceive their day-to-day progress in school. Also check in with their teachers (and administrators, when necessary). Use homework time as an opportunity to identify problem areas to address with teachers. If you detect any significant "slips" or "leaps" in a foster child's educational progress, bring these changes to the teacher's attention.

CROSS-CULTURAL TRAINING

Cross-cultural (or *transcultural* or *transracial*) foster parenting refers to the placement of a foster child of one race or ethnic group with a foster family of a different race or ethnic group. Cross-cultural foster parenting is common, not only because it fills a societal need, but also because most people who become foster parents are interested in caring for children from all cultural, ethnic, and racial backgrounds, not just their own.

Because cross-cultural fostering is so common, a fair number of foster care agencies and other organizations hold foster parent training courses on the subject. Such training classes usually include useful information about specific ways that foster parents can help preserve the customs and traditions of foster children from different cultural backgrounds. There are also resources that offer practical tips on very specific cross-cultural topics, such as teaching non–African American foster or adoptive parents how to style African American children's hair.

One example of a cross-cultural training course is "Parenting Across Racial and Cultural Lines," which is an online class for foster parents offered by FosterClub.com, www.fosterclub.com/grownups/index.cfm. The North American Council on Adoptable Children (NACAC; www.nacac.org) also holds frequent trainings and seminars on the subject of cross-cultural fostering and adopting.

MENTORING NEW FOSTER PARENTS

New and prospective foster parents have always turned to experienced foster parents for guidance, wisdom, and emotional support. Some programs formalize this tradition by providing mentors with training in specific areas, so that the mentors can be of even greater service to new foster parents.

One such organization, the Nebraska-based FOCUS (Families Offering Care, Understanding, and Support), which helps foster care agencies and organizations create effective mentoring programs for foster families, describes a mentor in its manual. It defines a mentor as "a caring person who offers support, guidance, and encouragement." The manual goes on to say, "Mentors offer assistance to families by helping them find their way through the daily challenges they may face by offering their knowledge and experience in a foster care or adoption system." In one sense, a mentor functions as a friend who "has the time to listen and give thoughtful feedback to the problem or concern."

If you would like to read the FOCUS program manual, "Mentoring for Foster and Adoptive Families," it is available at NFPAonline.org.

Your state foster parent organization may be able to match you up with an appropriate mentor, or—at a later date—to help you become a mentor yourself. Generally speaking, the most effective foster parenting mentors tend to have a manner that is professional, positive, wise, and patient. They should enjoy interacting with others and should be knowledgeable about specific foster parenting organizations, community resources, and the foster care system in general.

FOSTER PARENT SUPPORT GROUPS

The formal training you receive before and during the time you serve as a foster parent is valuable to your growth and development as a foster parent. The support you get from your fellow foster parents in a support group is equally important. The caseworkers at your foster care agency or representatives at your state foster parent association will be able to tell you when and where your local foster parent support group meets.

If you have ever participated in a support group, you know that group members sit together and talk about anything and everything pertaining to the topic at hand. People tend to talk about their most pressing issues and concerns, sometimes just to vent, but often to find out what others have done in similar situations. Foster parent support groups provide an open forum for exchanging information and ideas about the joys and challenges of foster parenting. Confidentiality is always paramount, so most participants take great care to talk in generalities and to leave names out of the conversation.

The people in your foster parent support group will understand everything you are going through in a way that other people in your life, no matter how well intentioned, simply cannot. After all, your fellow foster parents are the only ones who have walked in your shoes.

KEY CHAPTER CONCEPTS

- As "professional parents," foster parents benefit from training. Many states require participation in orientations, preservice training, *and* ongoing in-service training classes.

- Preservice training often includes instruction in child development and in effective communication. This training also helps foster parents learn to deal with ongoing home visits and with foster children's biological parents.

- In-service training can include workshops on subjects of special interest to foster parents and their families, such as dealing with ADHD or helping children with disabilities. It can also include advocacy training and cross-cultural training.

- As a new foster parent, you can learn not only from formal classes and workshops but also from mentors and other parents in support groups.

5

THE FINANCIALS OF FOSTERING

Potential foster parents should have realistic expectations of all aspects of foster parenting, including the financial aspect. This chapter will walk you through the essential financial realities, so you can consider whether fostering will work for you.

Above all, you should understand two very important things.

First, foster parents are volunteers who serve the foster care system. They are not paid employees. The money they receive for foster children is not categorized as a wage or salary, but as a reimbursement or stipend for the maintenance costs of caring for, housing, feeding, and clothing foster children.

Second, the reimbursement will probably not cover all foster parenting expenses. In most states, the reimbursement rates offered are lower than the real cost of caring for a child and are predetermined on a yearly basis by each county or state.

What does this all add up to? As a potential foster parent, you do not have to be wealthy, but you do have to be in a financial position to support your family *without* the addition of foster children to your household. During the application process, you will be required to prove that you have a steady, reliable, and adequate income.

FEDERAL AND STATE FUNDING

The Social Security Act, which was enacted in its earliest form in 1935, pertains to many different groups of people, including children in foster care. It has been amended many times since it was first passed, each time to reflect the ever-changing needs of the various citizens it was designed to serve.

IV-E: THE PRIMARY FUNDING SOURCE FOR FOSTER CARE

One relevant section of the Social Security Act is Title IV—Grants to States for Aid and Services to Needy Families with Children and for Child–Welfare Services. Part E of Title IV (generally known as IV-E) is the part of the Social Security Act that is of the greatest interest to foster parents and potential foster parents.

Section 470 of Title IV-E grants federal monies to states to fund the ongoing administration of state and county foster care programs. Section 472 of Title IV-E, which describes the Foster Care Maintenance Payments Program, explains in detail how the payment system from the federal government to the various state governments works.

The federal government is the primary source of funding for the care of foster children. State and local governments receive grants from the federal government to provide reimbursement or maintenance payments to foster parents.

If you are interested in reading more about the Social Security system as a whole, including its role in the lives of foster children, visit the main website, www.socialsecurity.gov.

If you are interested in reading Section 470 in its entirety, visit www.ssa.gov/OP_Home/ssact/title04/0470.htm.

If you are interested in reading Section 472 in its entirety, visit www.ssa.gov/OP_Home/ssact/title04/0472.htm.

DIFFERENT STATES, DIFFERENT COMPENSATION

Federal law mandates that all state and local child welfare agencies provide foster parents with reimbursement or maintenance funds to cover the basic costs of caring for children, such as food, shelter, and clothing. Typically, these reimbursement payments are funded from a combination of federal, state, and county resources. In October 2007, the National Foster Parent Association (NFPA) coauthored a landmark report called "Hitting the MARC: Establishing Foster Care Minimum Adequate Rates for Children," which revealed that states and counties have full discretion in setting the foster care reimbursement rates in their areas.

The report showed that monthly reimbursement rates varied widely, ranging from $226 per month in Nebraska to $869 per month in Washington, D.C. At the time the report was written, only Arizona and the District of Columbia provided foster parents with reimbursement rates that met or exceeded the standards established by the NFPA. The remaining states would have to raise their monthly rates by an average of 36 percent to meet the minimal standards established in the report.

Of course, the cost of living varies considerably from state to state, and the report's authors concede that this may account for some of the variability among rates from state to state. (The report's authors calculated and proposed appropriate monthly reimbursement rate increases that take each state's cost-of-living figures into account.) Nonetheless, the range is too great for cost of living to be the sole cause of this variability.

The authors of "Hitting the MARC" suggest another possible cause: "Low among myriad state and local budget priorities, foster care rates in many states do not appear to be based on a real assessment of children's basic needs." Consequently, in most states, the rates fall far short of the amount of money foster parents actually need to care adequately for a child.

You can access the NFPA's "Hitting the MARC" report in its entirety at www.childrensrights.org. You can find your state's proposed rate increase for each age group of children in foster care by visiting this page and clicking on the link to your state.

As a prospective foster parent, it is important to be aware of this financial information before you decide whether to become a foster parent. It may have some bearing on your decision.

When foster parents do not have enough money to cover additional costs out-of-pocket, it is the foster children who suffer, because they miss out on activities and opportunities. Low monthly reimbursement rates also have a negative effect on foster parent recruitment and retention. After all, when foster parents find that they cannot make ends meet while fostering, they often stop accepting new placements. When people stop fostering because they cannot afford to continue, this increases children's chances of being moved excessively from one living arrangement to another or of being placed in institutional settings or group homes rather than in family homes.

EXCEPTIONAL CIRCUMSTANCES

There are some exceptional circumstances in which foster care reimbursement or maintenance rates could be higher than average. Foster parents who provide "therapeutic foster care" or who care for foster children who are considered "medically fragile" often receive a higher rate of reimbursement. The costs associated with caring for these children tend to be significantly greater than the costs of caring for other foster children.

Therapeutic foster care is intensive care provided in a family home that operates within the guidelines of a residential treatment facility or as an adjunct to a mental health facility, and for which a fee is paid to specially trained foster parents. The children who receive this kind of foster care have been determined by the state to have physical, emotional, behavioral, or mental health needs that cannot be adequately met by their biological parents, in a group home, or in a traditional foster family setting.

A medically fragile foster child is one whose physical condition, as documented by the child's pediatrician, may become unstable and change in an instant, thereby triggering a life-threatening situation. Children with feeding tubes, respiratory tubes, shunts, tracheotomies, sleep apnea, severe diabetes, or other similar physical impairments are considered "medically fragile."

Foster care agencies that place medically fragile children recruit foster parents who are interested in this kind of fostering, regardless of their level of fostering experience. Often nurses, some of whom have no previous foster parenting experience, train to take care of medically fragile children. Many individuals interested in fostering medically fragile children go through a preservice training program before accepting their first placement.

WHAT FOSTER CARE FUNDING COVERS

According to Title IV-E of the Social Security Act, foster care maintenance payments are intended to cover "the cost of (and the cost of providing) food, clothing, shelter, daily supervision, school supplies, a child's personal incidentals, liability insurance with respect to a child, and reasonable travel to the child's home for visitation."

With very few exceptions, the federal Medicaid program covers nearly all of the health-care expenses of children in the foster care system. As a foster parent, you will be provided with a foster child's Medicaid card to present in medical, dental, and counseling offices on the child's behalf, and you will not be asked to make any copayments upon completion of medical appointments.

For more detailed information about the services provided by the Medicaid program, see the main Medicaid website: www.cms.hhs.gov.

WHAT'S NOT COVERED

Many expenses associated with caring for foster children are not funded. For example, the phrase "daily supervision" does *not* refer to the cost of day care or babysitters. Foster parents who work and must find care for their foster children during work hours are obliged to cover the cost of that day care or babysitting out-of-pocket. (Note that these alternative care providers must be approved and licensed by the child's foster care agency, even though it doesn't pay for them.)

In addition, dues and other costs for extracurricular activities such as sports, drama clubs, art programs, Scout troops, and other after-school activities tend not to be covered. Therefore, expenses associated with any of these activities are generally paid for by the child's foster parents. Most foster parents of school-age children will face some of these expenses, as participating in such programs and activities can be an integral part of making a child feel at home and involved in a community.

Other unanticipated expenses may arise. For instance, you may find it necessary to buy a larger vehicle to provide transportation for all of the children living with you. Gasoline is covered only if it is used to transport foster children to and from the homes of their biological families for visits, so the gas costs you will incur driving your foster children to school, activities, and appointments are your responsibility.

EDUCATION COSTS

Most children in foster care attend public school, which means no tuition costs are incurred by the foster parents. If a foster child in your care has special educational needs, these needs must be met by the public schools in your community. You may have to advocate on behalf of the foster children in your care to make sure that they are receiving the testing and other special educational services they require. You may also need to have a role (along with the child's caseworker, teachers, and school administrators) in creating, or perhaps modifying, a child's Individualized Education Program (IEP), which customizes a school's curriculum to address special needs such as ADHD, dyslexia, and learning disabilities.

Finally, if you wish to hire a tutor to provide additional academic assistance to a particular foster child, you may have to pay for this out-of-pocket. You can try to petition the child's foster care agency for financial assistance, but remember that the monthly reimbursement rate for foster children is a predetermined figure that in most cases cannot be altered or increased upon a foster parent's request. If you feel a tutor would be beneficial for the foster child, it's a good idea to ask teachers and administrators at the child's school if they can recommend skilled tutors who charge reasonable rates.

RECEIVING MAINTENANCE PAYMENTS

As a foster parent, you will receive a set monthly amount that has been predetermined by your state or municipality. It is your responsibility to use all the funds you receive to cover the costs of caring for the foster children in your care. You will generally receive this payment, which will be sent via your foster care agency, in the form of a monthly check. The first payment is typically issued "in arrears," that is, between 30 and 45 days after the child has been placed in the foster family's home.

Because the reimbursement in your area is predetermined, you will *not* be required to submit receipts or other paperwork associated with foster care expenditures to the foster care agency or any other governmental agency. However, you will likely be encouraged by your foster care agency to keep a folder containing such paperwork as part of your own financial records.

KEY CHAPTER CONCEPTS

- Foster parents are volunteers who do not earn wages or a salary for their services, but rather receive reimbursement for the maintenance costs of caring for foster children.

- In most states and localities, the monthly foster care reimbursement rates are lower than the true cost of caring for a child. While potential foster parents do not have to be wealthy, they do have to be in a financial position to support their family without the addition of foster children to the household.

- The federal funding program (known as Title IV-E) is the principal funding source for the U.S. foster care system. State and local governments receive grants from this program to provide reimbursement or maintenance payments to foster parents. However, there are widespread disparities among monthly state reimbursement rates.

- Reimbursement funds are intended to cover the cost of the foster child's food, clothing, shelter, daily supervision, school supplies, personal incidentals, liability insurance, and travel costs to and from the home of the child's biological family for visits. Medicaid covers health, dental, and counseling costs.

- Reimbursement payments for foster children do not include the cost of day care or babysitters. Nor do they include the costs of after-school activities, educational tutoring, or other miscellaneous items.

6

YOUR FIRST PLACEMENT

Once you have been approved to serve as a foster parent, you will receive an official letter or certificate in the mail from your foster care agency informing you that you are eligible. Sometime after this you'll receive a phone call from the agency regarding your very first placement.

It's natural to be both nervous and excited about your first placement. All of us can feel a little ambivalent when the thing we've wished for is about to come true. That's why we've devoted this entire chapter to this special experience.

KEY CONCERNS AND ISSUES

The application process you have just completed has been very rigorous. At this stage in your journey, you're familiar with the foster care system in general and with your agency in particular.

One or more staff members from the agency will have visited with you in your home on one or even several occasions. You will have completed initial orientation sessions as well as your preservice training. In addition, you will have had numerous opportunities to ask questions of caseworkers, foster parent trainers, home certifiers, and experienced foster parents.

So do keep in mind that, even though you're still new to the world of foster care, you've come a long way from the first day you said to yourself, "I think I might make a good foster parent. Maybe I'll look into it and give it a try."

Something else worth remembering is that your foster care agency wants all of your placements, including your first placement, to be successful. You are all on the same team! Agency staff members know you well from the application and training process, and they will use all the data they have gathered to match you up with a child they believe you can work with and help.

DO YOU HAVE A CHOICE?

Your first placement, like all subsequent placements, will involve a mutual agreement between you and your foster care agency that a particular child will join your family. *You do have a choice* about each and every placement.

A caseworker will call you to discuss a particular child's history and needs. If, for whatever reason, you have doubts about the placement, you should tell the caseworker that you don't think you would be a good match for that particular child at that time. However, these decisions require a great deal of thought, so don't be too hasty to say no.

Some new foster parents may have a preconceived image of the first foster child they will care for. For instance, you may be thinking, "I'd like my first placement to be a girl under the age of five with little history of behavioral problems." Instead, the caseworker on the telephone says that the actual child in need of your care right now is a 12-year-old boy with a history of acting out under stress.

There's no need to panic. You are well within your rights to ask the caseworker if you can think about it, discuss it with your partner, and then call back within a reasonable time frame. Have faith in your training and parenting skills. After all, you have worked extremely hard to prepare yourself and your family to provide excellent foster care to boys and girls of all ages.

If you're mulling over the possibility of fostering a child with behavioral issues—especially if this is not what you pictured ahead of time—consider this: *You decided to become a foster parent to help children in need.* For a variety of reasons—including upset over separation from their biological parents or possible repercussions from abuse or neglect—many children in need of foster care have behavioral issues. If you have reached this point in the preparation and training process, you are clearly up for a serious challenge—and the agency thinks you are, too.

Remember the useful tips and strategies you learned in your training, as well as from parenting your own children, if you have them. Think of the value of employing these tips and strategies. The children you foster can benefit from the example of compassion and strength you set and will have an enormous sense of pride and autonomy once they learn how to better manage their emotions. The lessons you teach will not only serve them during the time they live in your home, but in future situations as well.

If you agree to foster a child with behavioral challenges, you'll doubtless have some—perhaps even many—difficult moments. Perhaps some of the tools you offer will not become part of that child's personal toolbox. But perhaps some of them will, and that possibility should give you hope.

The choice is yours. But saying yes to the unanticipated might be one of the best things ever to happen to a child in need of your nurturing care. It could turn out to be a profoundly enriching experience for you, too.

A FIRST PLACEMENT THAT WORKED

In the foreword of this book, longtime foster mother and former National Foster Parent Association (NFPA) president Shirley Hedges talks about her first placement. As she explains, she and her husband had been hoping to foster a young child when she received her first placement 32 years ago. Their own biological daughters were six and three, and they thought another young child might be a perfect fit for their family at that stage in their lives.

But the call that came was a request for Shirley and her husband to foster an 11-year-old girl who had run away from home and had been absent from school for several weeks. Did this correspond with the mental picture that the Hedgeses then had? Certainly not! Nevertheless, this first placement turned out to be a wonderful success story for all involved. This particular child stayed in permanent foster care with the Hedgeses from the age of 11 to the age of 19, while continuing to have positive visits with her biological family. She was 43 years old when this book was written and still in regular contact with the Hedgeses and several members of her biological family.

Stories like this one are powerful reminders of what a positive force fostering can be in the lives of the child, the foster family, and the biological family. Not every foster care story works out this beautifully, but real-life stories just like this one can give you some idea of what is possible when good-hearted people work toward the shared goal of bettering the lives of children in need. Before you make a difficult decision about whether or not to take a child, seek the counsel of foster families who have walked the walk.

THE PLACEMENT PROCESS

When determining where to place children, caseworkers will consider everything they know about the children and about you. The caseworker has met you and is familiar with you from the application and assessment process. He or she has seen where and how you live. He or she has had heart-to-heart talks with you about your own upbringing and about your views on parenting. He or she has a good idea of your temperament and tolerance level—not to mention your sense of compassion and your sense of humor.

In addition, the caseworker knows the children in question and how much they struggle when they have to change families, homes, neighborhoods, and schools. So the challenge for the caseworker is to imagine how a particular child will function in your home, how this child will mesh with you and your family when you are all living under the same roof. The caseworker will offer you as much information as possible about the child you might foster so you can make an informed decision about whether it is a good match. It's not in the caseworker's interest to hold anything back, since he or she wants to make sure you understand the child and the child's needs and doesn't want the placement to fail.

But no matter how much you are told, you may wish to know more, and this is the best time to ask as many questions as you can think of. Of course, you can continue to ask questions after the child is placed with you, but the more you understand up front, the smoother the adjustment is likely to be for all of you.

PREPLACEMENT MEETINGS

After your caseworker tells you about a potential placement and you agree to the match, they will tell the child about you. Caseworkers prepare foster children for placement by answering their questions and giving them the information they'll need to understand the family they are about to join. The caseworker will describe your family, your home, and your neighborhood.

If the child's biological family is going to be involved in the child's care team, the caseworker will be thinking ahead about a plan for family visits. Prior to the placement, depending upon the policies and procedures of your particular foster care agency, you may have the opportunity to meet with the child and even the child's biological family.

The meeting might take place in the caseworker's office or in your home. Meeting in your home is particularly beneficial. It can give the child an initial impression of family life in your household, and it can give you a sense of how things may work out if ultimately you do serve as the child's foster parent.

In some instances, you may have more than one pre-care meeting before the official placement occurs. In this way, you, the child, the caseworker, and the biological family (if appropriate) will have the chance to get to know each other and gradually build a rapport. If the child is not in an emergency situation that necessitates immediate placement, multiple pre-care meetings can be a helpful preparation tool for all involved.

PREPARING YOURSELF AND YOUR FAMILY

In a sense, you have been preparing yourself for this moment all along. Everything you have done up until this point to educate yourself about foster parenting has been about building up your understanding and your confidence. You have read books and articles about foster care, participated in orientation sessions and training, and talked to your caseworker and experienced foster parents, all to make sure you are ready to face the first moments of the first day of your first placement.

You are far more prepared than you may even realize. Remember, first and foremost, foster parenting stems from the desire to help children in need. Clearly you have this desire, or you would not be this far along in the process. Keep your expectations reasonable, and believe in yourself and in your potential to help foster children.

Just as you have been preparing yourself throughout the application and assessment process, you have also been preparing your partner and children. Most of your family members' questions have probably been asked and answered, but here are a few additional tips from foster care experts.

ALLOW TIME TO ADJUST

Foster children require time and space to get acclimated to a new home. They are bound to feel some anxiety even if they have already met you and your family. You and your family members will also be experiencing some anxiety mixed in with eager anticipation and excitement. Just remember that the nervousness is simply part of facing the new and unknown.

YOUR CHILDREN ARE ROLE MODELS

If you have other children, they will be role models for all the foster children who enter your home. Your foster children will look to your children for guidance and clues as to how children in this household are expected to behave. Children are naturally good at imitation, which is a profoundly effective survival mechanism. Foster children will begin to take pride and pleasure in imitating your children's good behavior, in large part because it inspires positive feedback from you and your partner.

If your biological children are on board with the idea of serving as role models, this can be beneficial to everyone. It will make your children feel that they have important roles in the foster child's life, and it will inspire them to be at their best. And the bottom line is the better your children behave, the better the foster children will behave.

One caveat: Researchers have found that not all biological children of foster parents enjoy the idea of serving as role models to foster children, so be sure to discuss this topic with your own children at length. If they are not comfortable with the idea of being role models, assure them that you understand and respect their feelings, and that you and your partner will be happy to serve as the foster children's primary behavioral role models. Pressuring your children at this time could be counterproductive. They may need extra time to adapt to the situation without feeling that they are risking disappointing you. (Chapter 13 will further address the various ways in which fostering can affect your existing family.)

NURTURE CHANNELS OF COMMUNICATION

Remind your partner and your children that the dialogue you are having about what it means to be a foster family is an *ongoing conversation*. This is not a dialogue that will come to a halt when a foster child comes to live with you. Let your family know that you are always happy and available to listen to them about any questions or concerns they may have about being a foster family.

TREAT ALL YOUR CHILDREN FAIRLY

When you become a foster family, it is essential to treat everyone in the household fairly and equally. For example, regarding chores and rules, no one child should have to do more or less than any other child. If your children and the foster children in your care feel that they are being treated equally, you will create an atmosphere of peace and harmony.

Be sure to heed your foster care agency's directives regarding discipline of your foster children. Most agencies state that discipline must be appropriate to a child's age and special needs. Cruel, severe, or unusual punishment is not tolerated under any circumstances. Corporal punishment of any kind is forbidden. Deprivation of meals, isolation in excess of one hour, and verbal abuse, threats, and humiliation are strictly prohibited.

You should apply disciplinary standards equally to all the children in your home. If a foster child is not allowed to, say, eat snacks outside of the kitchen or watch television before homework is done, other children shouldn't be allowed to do these things, either.

TALK ABOUT APPROPRIATE VS. INAPPROPRIATE TOUCH

You have probably already talked with your own children about the differences between "appropriate touch" and "inappropriate touch," but not all foster children have been fortunate enough to have had such conversations with a caring adult. Moreover, some foster children have been physically or sexually abused in the past. Children who have been neglected or victimized do not always have a clear understanding of the differences between appropriate and inappropriate touch. They may think it is acceptable to hit or pinch or bite, for instance, because they have been hit or pinched or bitten in the past.

Similarly, they may think it is acceptable to touch other people in their private areas because they have been touched inappropriately in the past. This is one reason why foster families need to be compassionate, patient, and nonjudgmental. Remember, children cannot know that a particular behavior is inappropriate unless they are taught that it is inappropriate and that there are alternative, appropriate ways to behave and to express affection.

You can certainly take some practical, realistic steps to prevent such problems. Probably the most effective strategy is to provide close monitoring and supervision of your children and any foster children in your care. Supervision is the best preventive measure; after all, children who are well supervised by caring adults do not have much opportunity to do the wrong thing. Many foster children even enjoy the attention and sense of safety and nurturing that close supervision provides because many of them have suffered neglect as well as abuse. When you pay them attention and provide positive feedback, they feel cared for, nurtured, and valued.

Finally, remind your children to firmly say "No!" if a foster child is infringing on their space or seems to be on the brink of doing something inappropriate, verbally or physically. As simple as it may sound, a firmly stated "No!" can work wonders to help your children and foster children respect each other's physical and emotional space and boundaries.

PREPARING YOUR HOME

In many ways, your home will already be prepared for your first placement because it will have been thoroughly inspected and you will have made any necessary changes requested by the home assessor. For instance, if you have been approved to foster infants and toddlers, you will have already baby-proofed your home and installed car seats in your vehicles. Regardless of how many preplacement visits occur, however, it is your responsibility to make sure that your home is safe and welcoming for children.

GATHERING STAPLES

You can lay the foundation for a strong relationship by providing the foster children in your care with some of their favorite foods and toys. Seeing these familiar items when they first come to live with you will help them feel at home. Moreover, they will appreciate the effort you have made to find out what they enjoy and obtain those things. Feel free to ask about favorite foods and toys during your preplacement meetings with the child, the caseworker, and the child's biological parents.

When it comes to clothing, outer garments, and shoes, it might be advisable to wait until the foster child is living with you to accumulate most of what they'll need. Depending on the age of the child, you can go to stores together and find styles the child likes. In addition, you can make sure the clothes, coats, and shoes fit properly and are appropriate for school.

SPECIAL EQUIPMENT

If you have trained to become a foster parent of medically fragile children, the first child placed in your home may require special medical equipment. You will be taught how to use, clean, and maintain this equipment, and medical personnel familiar with the child's specific medical situation will provide you with the appropriate training you will need. Once again, it is imperative that you ask questions about anything you do not fully understand.

SUPPORT FROM THE FOSTER CARE AGENCY

Your foster care agency will play an integral role in preparing you, your family, the foster child, and the child's biological family for the life-altering transition that a foster care placement inevitably heralds.

CASEWORKERS PREPARE THE BIOLOGICAL FAMILY

Social workers and other staff members who work for foster care agencies realize that the removal of a child from the biological parents' home is a traumatic experience not only for the child, but also for the biological parents. They know that birth parents need time and space to process any feelings of anger, sadness, guilt, or embarrassment over their child being placed in out-of-home care.

Caseworkers receive special training in how to help biological parents manage their grief and anger and also to help them learn how to channel these negative feelings into positive efforts to change and be reunified with their child one day. Caseworkers are trained to explain to the biological parents exactly what they must do in order to be reunited with their child.

For several reasons, it is essential—whenever possible and appropriate—to include the biological parents in planning for their child's future. This sends them the crucial message that they are an important part of the child's care team, that they are respected by both the agency workers and the foster parents, and that their opinions are valued. Finally, being involved in their child's permanency planning gives them a powerful incentive to change their ways and be reunited with their child.

CASEWORKERS PREPARE THE CHILD

Children suffer deeply when they are taken away from their biological parents, even in situations where the parents have been abusive or neglectful. In most instances, the children will feel a mixture of grief, sorrow, sadness, fear, and abandonment. Some children also experience feelings of guilt because they incorrectly believe that they have done something wrong and are being punished. The job of the caseworker and the foster parents is to make every effort to explain to these children why they are being removed from their homes. In this way, they will be less saddened, shocked, and frightened when the actual removal takes place.

Ideally, the child will have had the chance to meet with his or her caseworker on several occasions so that the two of them can start to build a rapport before the child is removed from the biological parents' home. There are exceptions, however, such as when a child is removed from a home on an emergency basis.

It is also traumatic for children to be placed in a new and unfamiliar home, which is why preplacement visits between child and foster family are considered so important and beneficial. They help the child and the foster family to feel more emotionally prepared for the placement and reduce everyone's anxiety level.

CASEWORKERS PREPARE THE FOSTER FAMILY

Caseworkers provide foster families with the background information they need about the foster child, including medical, behavioral, and educational information. They also inform foster families about the agency's policies regarding child discipline.

Caseworkers are also required to keep foster parents apprised of all permanency planning issues, including any changes in the permanency plan as the placement progresses. For instance, the caseworker may initiate a dialogue with the foster family about becoming a foster child's permanent family if it turns out that the child cannot be reunited with his biological parents and there are no appropriate permanent kinship care options for the child.

KEY CHAPTER CONCEPTS

- Many new foster parents feel anxious and wonder what to expect from their first foster care placements. However, even if the reality of your first placement does not exactly match your expectations, remember you have been training for this day for a long time and you are much more prepared than you think.

- Caseworkers try to ensure successful placements by matching children in need with appropriate foster families, sharing information, answering questions, and arranging for pre-care meetings.

- It is important to prepare yourself, your family, and your house for your first foster care placement. Providing some of the foster child's favorite foods and toys can help the child feel welcome.

- It's important to be emotionally as well as physically prepared: give foster children time and space to adjust, encourage your biological children to be role models, and talk to your children about "appropriate touch" versus "inappropriate touch."

- Before and during the placement process, caseworkers help prepare all parties involved. They inform birth parents why their children are being removed from their custody and what they can do to regain custody, they give foster parents as much history as possible about the children, and they arrange for preplacement visits to help foster parents and foster children get acquainted.

7

FOSTERING INFANTS AND TODDLERS, 0–3

What is it like to care for the youngest children in foster care? This chapter describes the typical developmental milestones for healthy infants and toddlers, as well as problems that can prevent some foster children from reaching these milestones on schedule.

You'll also learn why many infants and toddlers in foster families struggle to bond with the adults who care for them. Practical tips from child-development experts will provide you with the tools you need to help foster infants and toddlers overcome potential bonding and adjustment struggles.

DEVELOPMENTAL MILESTONES

What is typical behavior for a young child? There is certainly room for variation in normal development. Nevertheless, if you are a foster parent of an infant or toddler, it can be useful to consult a checklist that describes when most young children reach certain benchmarks.

The following list, while not completely comprehensive, can help you recognize what to expect. If the baby or toddler in your care does not meet these usual milestones, it *might* be a sign that he or she needs special attention. In such cases, a professional opinion would be useful.

At 3 months of age, most babies ...

- Turn their heads toward bright colors and lights.
- Move both eyes in the same direction.
- Recognize the bottle or breast.
- React to sudden sounds or voices.
- Make cooing sounds.
- Make fists with both hands.
- Grasp toys or hair.
- Wiggle and kick with arms and legs.
- Are able to lift their heads and chests when on their stomachs.
- Smile.

At 6 months of age, most babies ...

- Follow moving objects with their eyes.
- Turn toward the source of normal sounds.
- Reach for objects and pick them up.
- Switch toys from one hand to the other.
- Play with their toes.
- Help hold their bottle during feedings.
- Recognize familiar faces.
- Babble.

At 12 months of age, most babies ...

- Sit without support.
- Pull up to a standing position.
- Crawl.
- Drink from a cup.

- Play peek-a-boo and patty-cake.
- Wave bye-bye.
- Hold out their arms and legs while being dressed.
- Put objects in a container.
- Stack two blocks.
- Know five or six words.

At 18 months of age, most toddlers …

- Like to pull, push, and dump things.
- Follow simple directions ("Bring the ball").
- Pull off their shoes, socks, and mittens.
- Like to look at pictures.
- Make marks on paper with crayons.
- Walk without help.
- Can step off a low object and keep their balance.

At 2 years of age, most toddlers …

- Create two- to three-word sentences ("Give milk!").
- Say names of toys.
- Recognize familiar pictures.
- Carry something while walking.
- Feed themselves with a spoon.
- Play independently.
- Turn two to three pages of a book at a time.
- Like to imitate their parents.
- Can identify their hair, eyes, ears, and nose by pointing.
- Can build a tower of four blocks.
- Readily show affection.

At 3 years of age, most toddlers …

- Walk up steps (alternating feet).
- Ride a tricycle.
- Put on their shoes.
- Open doors.
- Turn one page of a book at a time (indicating improved fine motor control).
- Play with other children for a few minutes.
- Repeat common rhymes.
- Use three- to five-word sentences.
- Name at least one color correctly.
- Are toilet-trained or on their way to being toilet-trained.

Don't expect too much from infants and toddlers at each stage. Sentences won't be grammatically perfect, and feeding themselves with a spoon won't involve Miss Manners–like table etiquette. But if a foster infant or toddler in your care does not seem to be developing according to the basic milestones described above, you should contact the child's caseworker and pediatrician about getting a referral for the early intervention program in your county. Studies show that the earlier children enter programs to address developmental delays, the better the prognosis.

HOW TRAUMA CAN AFFECT CHILD DEVELOPMENT

Researchers have found that normal development can be disrupted when infants and toddlers witness violence or have themselves been the victims of violence. For instance, very young children who witness or experience violence in their homes may have more sleep problems; regress developmentally; become more irritable, fearful, aggressive, withdrawn, or clingy; and even show signs of early-onset *post-traumatic stress disorder (PTSD)*. Such experiences can also impair children's cognitive development, causing them to score lower on intelligence tests than nontraumatized children.

However, it is important to note that not all victimized children respond in such self-defeating ways. Researchers have found that many young children are astoundingly resilient.

Indeed, the first three years of a child's life present an unparalleled opportunity for caring foster parents. Proactive intervention during these early years can exponentially improve the lives of foster infants and toddlers. Most young children respond positively to being nurtured, protected, and taught how to cope with their feelings and behaviors.

> **Post-traumatic stress disorder (PTSD)** is an anxiety disorder caused by serious traumatic events and characterized by such symptoms as reliving the trauma in nightmares, feeling emotional numbness, and/or experiencing recurrent intrusive thoughts or images of the trauma.

BONDING CHALLENGES

The primary developmental task of all infants and toddlers is to form healthy emotional attachments to their birth parents or their other primary care providers, such as their foster parents. Indeed, early proponents of *attachment theory* (the study of humans' emotional bonding behavior) John Bowlby and Mary Ainsworth noted in their research that between birth and three years of age, young children are hard at work forming profound emotional attachments to their parents. For instance, babies often watch their parents with great intensity and may smile or coo or become calm and peaceful in their presence. Bonding is, quite literally, the "job" of the very young child. And parents can facilitate this job.

However, children who have been abused or neglected by their biological parents can have difficulty developing trust and forming healthy, secure attachments to the new adults caring for them. Consistency is a major component of healthy attachment. Unfortunately, many infants and toddlers in the foster care system have experienced multiple disruptions in the course of their brief lives. Initially, they are removed from their biological parents' homes, usually as a direct consequence of parental neglect or abuse. Then, for a variety of reasons, they may be moved again and again, from one foster home to another.

Originally described by the British scholar and researcher John Bowlby, **attachment theory** holds that infants and toddlers seek to bond closely with a parent (or other adult care provider) and tend to feel the safest and most secure when that person is close by. Attachment theory proponents call this bond "secure attachment." They maintain that children who feel a particularly strong emotional connection with their caregivers during childhood will be able to create and maintain secure, caring, mutually supportive relationships when they reach adulthood.

As you might expect, such multiple losses, disruptions, and transitions can be extremely confusing and upsetting—even traumatizing—for the children. With each new placement, foster children must adjust again to new sets of family dynamics, routines, and personalities. Confusion, frustration, or withdrawal may result.

HIGH-NEED BABIES AND TODDLERS

Many babies and toddlers in foster care are considered "high-need." They require more patience and attention and are fussier and more demanding than other babies. And they can drain their caregivers' energy.

Every time a high-need baby cries out, for example, it sounds like the baby is in urgent, desperate need of your immediate attention. The shrill summons can resemble a teakettle on continual boil. Some high-need babies and toddlers also tend to be hyperactive and demanding. Many of them feed more often and awaken during the night more frequently than other babies.

Many high-need babies crave the security of near-constant human touch. They want to be cuddled and held day and night. They can get quite upset when they are put down in their cribs, which can result in sleep deprivation for the entire household. On the other hand, some high-need babies do *not* like to be held and are not inclined to cuddle with their caregivers. This scenario is unsettling in its own way, for caregivers may feel rebuffed.

Finally, most high-need babies are separation-sensitive. They hate being apart from their primary caregivers, and it takes them a long time to warm up to new people. Leaving such children with sitters or in day care can be emotionally taxing for everyone concerned.

HELPING ATTACHMENT ALONG

An infant who is struggling in foster care may be experiencing emotional difficulties and bonding problems, often due to abuse or neglect suffered at the hands of the biological parents. What can you do as a foster parent to minimize the stress level of these young children? How can you help young foster children develop a healthy, secure, trusting attachment to you?

First and foremost, you can provide the nurturing, consistent care, and attention that these young children so desperately need. Your commitment to caring for young children for as long as they need to remain in foster care is critical for their emotional, physical, and psychological health and development.

In addition, experts cite several practical ways to comfort struggling infants:

- Hold them. Many foster infants and toddlers will love to be held by you, and studies show that babies and young children who are held frequently and tenderly thrive both emotionally and physically.

- Try wrapping or "swaddling" the baby snugly—but not *too* snugly—in blankets (the way you might wrap a taco filling in a taco shell). Many infants find the safe, secure feeling that swaddling provides to be enormously comforting.

- Consider carrying the infant in a front pack, sling, or baby hammock. (Some people call this "wearing the baby.") Many babies, including many high-need babies, find the physical closeness, combined with the feel and sound of your heartbeat, profoundly comforting.

- Try placing a struggling, fussy baby in a vibrating bed, seat, or swing. Many, though not all, children find the motion of these vibrating seats and beds very relaxing. As always, pay close attention to each individual infant's cues to see if this technique is well received.

- Always talk in a calm, low, quiet, soothing tone of voice. Similarly, when you sing and read to a baby, do so quietly and calmly, always with the primary goal of reducing the child's overall anxiety level.

- At naptime and bedtime, dim the lights. A room that is too brightly lit can be overly stimulating for any child, and especially so for a child who has suffered any kind of trauma.

- Try playing soft, soothing music, such as lullabies or quiet classical music (pick Bach or Schubert over Tchaikovsky's *1812 Overture*) to help lull the baby to sleep.

- Consider giving babies and toddlers warm baths before bed.

- At naptime and at night—but also in general—try to avoid overstimulation. A blaring television or radio can cause sensory overload, which can be stressful for children who have experienced abuse, neglect, or other difficulties in the past.

Not all strategies work for all children. If you try one that seems to backfire, that doesn't mean there is anything wrong with you or what you did. It may just not be this baby's proverbial cup of tea. The foster infant or toddler will give you the feedback you need to adjust your calming strategies.

HELPING STRUGGLING CHILDREN SELF-SOOTHE

Children in nurturing home environments can learn how to soothe themselves when they feel anxious or out of sorts. For instance, many children quickly discover that if they hold a special blanket or a favorite stuffed animal, they can actually calm themselves—sometimes all the way to sleep.

If you notice that a foster child is developing an attachment to a stuffed toy, blanket, or similar object, honor the child's preference and make sure that the object is available to the child—especially at *times of transition*, such as bedtime or times when you are leaving the child in someone else's care. (Child psychologists actually refer to these comfort objects as "transitional objects," because they help ease children's feelings as they go from familiar to unfamiliar or stressful settings.)

If a child has brought along a comfort object from the home of his or her biological family, don't take it away. In fact, don't even be tempted to wash it unless it is unsanitary or unsafe. Its smells may be the only connection—but a powerful, primal one—that the baby has with his or her biological parents.

BUILDING CONFIDENCE AND STRENGTH

The years from birth to age three are the time when children first start to build up their senses of confidence and self-worth. If they continually receive positive, nurturing feedback and support from you, they will eventually learn to believe in themselves and their abilities.

Experts recommend that you identify specific strengths in all children, but perhaps especially in foster children. For instance, if foster toddlers in your care love to build towers with blocks—and clearly feel an enormous sense of pride and accomplishment when they do—always praise them enthusiastically for their wonderful block tower–building skills. If they enjoy feeding themselves, applaud their efforts, even if a few Cheerios end up dotting the floor.

SAFE, HEALTHY TOUCH

Although it can be difficult for foster children to bond because of past hurts, many foster parent trainers recommend that foster parents use healthy, appropriate forms of physical touch to enhance emotional security and attachment. Examples of healthy touch include …

- Cuddling young children during feedings and story time.
- Rocking them in a rocking chair to soothe them before bedtime and when they are upset.
- Brushing and arranging their hair.
- Giving them quick, gentle hugs.
- Giving them pats on the back.

On the subject of touch, however, it is important to remember that some foster children have suffered physical or sexual abuse. For this reason, it is essential for you to have full knowledge of the child's entire trauma history. In such circumstances, limited touch—such as a quick pat on the hand—is recommended. Just be sure to keep the contact safe and brief.

Always pay close attention to a foster child's responses to touch, and be sure to respond accordingly. For example, if you reach out to pat a child on the head, does he wince or shrink back as if he is afraid he might be struck? If so, modify your behavior. In addition, if a child's behavior causes you to suspect that he has experienced past abuse you do not know about, don't be afraid to ask the caseworker how best to address the situation. Remember that every foster child's caseworker is only a phone call away.

INTERPRETING ACTING OUT BEHAVIORS

Parental loss or separation is traumatic for children of all ages. But children at different stages of life have different reactions to being separated from their parents, as well as different coping methods. Infants and toddlers cannot place a parental loss or separation in any kind of context in their minds. They have *only* known their initial caregivers and have no one with whom to compare them. When they are separated from their biological parents—no matter how abusive or neglectful those caregivers may have been—babies and toddlers experience the separation as a confusing and profoundly traumatic loss.

Young children's natural feelings of attachment to and affection for their biological parents can become mixed up with various negative feelings, such as anger, sadness, and a sense of rejection or abandonment. But just because babies and young children cannot put their complex mixture of positive and negative feelings into words does not make their feelings any less meaningful to them—or to you, the foster parent caring for them.

Because of their lack of language skills, infants and toddlers are far more likely to *show* you how sad and lost they feel by acting out. In this age group, acting out can take various forms.

- Some grieving babies and toddlers erect an emotional wall between themselves and their foster parents, becoming quiet and withdrawn.

- Some may avoid physical contact, such as hugs, because in the past, close contact meant that they were being hurt.

- Some may instinctively feel that the less they invest in this new relationship with you, the less they will be hurt if the relationship is suddenly taken from them.

- Some may express their insecurity as anger: misbehaving and throwing repeated temper tantrums.

Your job as a foster parent is to continue reaching out, to demonstrate to your young foster children that there is no need for them to withdraw or to fight you. It is essential for you to understand where these behaviors are coming from. The young children in your care are not rejecting or punishing *you* if they withdraw or indulge in tantrums. They are just having difficulty coping with their perfectly understandable feelings of confusion, anxiety, and grief.

POSITIVE PARENTING TECHNIQUES

For much of human history, it was believed that the role of parents was strictly to correct imperfect behavior—to reign in children's supposed inclination to wreak havoc. But in recent times, the prevalent thinking has been that parents can and should take an active role in promoting and perpetuating constructive behaviors, of which children are more than capable.

Foster parents, and all parents, can use the techniques of positive parenting, some of which are outlined here, to help the children in their care develop good habits and proactive attitudes.

TURN OFF THE TV; TURN THE PAGE

Consider shutting off the television set so that you and any young children in your care can instead play age-appropriate games together, work on simple puzzles, build with blocks, dance together to cheerful music, or—perhaps best of all—read.

Studies show it's important to read to all children, including babies and toddlers. Not only does it stimulate their intellectual and emotional growth, but it also provides valuable together time. So make reading a big part of your naptime, nighttime, and other routines.

Reading aloud can have special resonance for young foster children. For example, it helps foster infants learn to recognize and respond to your voice. In addition, reading together with foster infants and toddlers provides an opportunity for appropriate, nurturing, physical closeness and cuddling. It also promotes feelings of attachment, security, and safety.

Reading to all toddlers, including foster toddlers, can be a lot of fun. Here are some specific tips to make it both an enjoyable and an educational experience:

- Invite the children to select the books they would like to read.

- Ask questions that will help them feel more involved in and excited about the story.

- Use varied voices and sounds to depict the characters and action unfolding in the story.

- Point out interesting details in the pictures: "See that big smile on the little boy's face?"

- Urge toddlers to tell you what they see in the book's illustrations.

- Invite them to "read" to you, that is, to tell you their own made-up stories based on a book's pictures.

Last but not least, be aware that *all* toddlers love and learn from repetition. They will ask you to read the same stories over and over again, and over time, they will naturally develop special favorites. You may feel like you have certain stories coming out of your ears. Those are the ones they appreciate the most!

HAVE REGULAR ROUTINES

All of the experts agree that foster parents should try to establish as many routines as possible, particularly routines related to morning, bedtime, and reading time. Children are profoundly comforted by steadiness, structure, and reliability, especially if they have not experienced much consistency before coming to live with you. The more quickly you can establish these routines, the more likely you are to see positive changes in a child's behavior.

OFFER REASONABLE CHOICES

There are many situations in which toddlers should not be allowed to make choices, but whenever possible, give young children choices. This can be a great way to make them feel empowered, and it can reduce power struggles between the two of you. When you give toddlers choices, you are appealing to their natural desire for autonomy. In fact, providing choices is considered one of the hallmarks of positive parenting or positive disciplining.

Of course, when it comes to toddlers, the choices should always be simple and age-appropriate. For example, allow a toddler to choose between wearing her sandals or her sneakers to the park on a warm day. This will cut back on potential conflicts and will make her feel powerful and independent, like a big girl.

REDIRECT UPSETS

All children get attached to things they like and can sometimes get upset if they have to share these things. If a child experiences frustration because, say, someone else is playing with a toy he wants, tell the child that you know it can be frustrating when someone is playing with a toy they want. Then explain that we can't always have what we want exactly when we want it. Finally, redirect the child toward a different toy that he also enjoys playing with. In other words, change the focus.

Another redirecting method that childcare experts recommend involves distracting the child by using childlike silliness and humor. If you can get a toddler to laugh by talking to him in a silly voice, he may soon lose interest in the toy he has been coveting and instead turn his attention to you.

BE PATIENT WITH POTTY LEARNING

Potty training is difficult even under the best of circumstances. It can be even more difficult for foster children, who may have been the victims of abuse or who may be struggling with various developmental or behavioral issues. Many child-development specialists advise foster parents to think about the process from a different perspective: as potty "learning" rather than potty "training."

Think about all that is involved! We are asking children to learn to read their body's signals, grasp that certain feelings mean that it is time to go to the bathroom, undo their snaps or pull down their pants, and sit down on (or stand in front of) the toilet—all in time to "go"! We are also asking them to understand the brand-new sensation of keeping their pants dry, a concept they have never had to focus on before. That's a lot for a young child to think about and accomplish.

So, these days, doctors ask parents to keep an open mind and be flexible. Not all toddlers are ready to start this important learning process at the same time. Doctors tell foster parents to pay close attention to the clues and signals that children send about their personal readiness. Some children might be ready by the age of two and a half; others may start the process later. Patience and compassion, as you well know, are vital to all aspects of foster parenting, but are perhaps particularly important during potty learning.

REPEAT SIMPLE HOUSEHOLD RULES

Older toddlers can start to grasp a limited number of simple rules, such as "No crossing the street by yourself." Just remember that you will have to keep repeating even simple rules over and over again for them to sink in. All children—but perhaps especially foster children—take comfort in the sense of routine that consistently stated and enforced rules provide.

Another positive parenting technique to use with toddlers involves making fun games out of obeying household rules. This could include singing a song as you and a toddler in your care clean up a messy playroom together. ("Clean up, clean up, everybody everywhere ...")

PRESENT A UNITED FRONT

Two-parent households should always be sure to present a united front regarding household rules. Any children in your care would be very confused if you and your partner were to establish and enforce different sets of household rules.

There certainly may come a moment when you and your partner have an honest disagreement about a parenting strategy or household rule, but you must agree to resolve your differences in private. Don't subject the child to your negotiations. Negotiate first and then stand firm together.

CARING COMMUNICATION

A young foster child who enters your household may be talking, starting to talk, or still preverbal. If the child is speaking, he or she may be garrulous or quiet. But one thing is for certain—whatever the child's communication level or style, you need to be a good communicator. It is part of your role as a foster parent to make yourself understood and help the children in your care make themselves understood.

SPEAK SIMPLY, BE DIRECT

It's helpful to communicate in simple, direct, concrete language. Even infants and toddlers can understand comforting sounds and soothing words. Keep your vocabulary age-appropriate and your tone gentle. Studies show that we communicate more of our emotions by tone of voice than by the words we choose.

Don't be tempted to raise your voice if you feel your message is not registering. Be patient and repeat what you are saying calmly. Little by little, pieces of your tenderly communicated message will start to sink in and help the child through his or her complicated transition process.

ENCOURAGE HEALTHY EXPRESSION OF FEELINGS

Even with small children, it is very helpful for adults to model the naming of feelings. In this way, children can learn early on that it is perfectly appropriate—and emotionally healthy—to discuss their feelings out loud, without any shame. For example, if a toddler is sad about ending a play date she is enjoying, you can say, "It makes you sad to say good-bye to your friend. It's okay to miss him. You will be happy when you see him again."

Try using reflecting responses to help children in your care learn how to identify and express their feelings. You can do this by saying something like "You seem so happy right now!" when a toddler is smiling about something. Your reflecting responses give young foster children the chance to agree or disagree with you and also to tell you, in their own words, why they feel the way they do.

For clues to a child's emotions, pay attention to body language. Often young children's gestures, postures, and facial expressions reveal what they are feeling inside. (The same goes for adults, by the way.) By helping children understand their body language, you help them identify and come to grips with their feelings. For example, if a toddler seems to be on the brink of throwing a tantrum, you can express your empathy and concern by saying, "You're trembling and your face is getting red. You look angry. Let's talk about what you're feeling and how I can help you feel better."

Perhaps most important of all, be a role model. The more you name your own feelings (sadness, anger, happiness, and so on), the more the children in your care will understand that not only is it acceptable to *have* feelings, but it is also acceptable to *talk about* these feelings. Perhaps the children came to you from homes where feelings were rarely, if ever, labeled or discussed. Or, worse yet, perhaps openly expressing emotion was viewed as a sign of vulnerability and weakness and was punished. If so, then learning from you that it's perfectly fine to experience and express feelings in words can be a wonderful revelation.

KEY CHAPTER CONCEPTS

- It's important that foster parents of infants and toddlers become familiar with typical developmental milestones. If a child in your care seems out of sync with his or her age group, seek a professional opinion.

- Many infants and toddlers in foster care struggle to bond with their foster parents. You can promote attachment through methods such as rocking, swaddling, and "wearing" infants, and by using appropriate touch—such as hugs and pats on the back—with toddlers.

- You can comfort anxious children with soothing sounds, dim lights, and warm baths before bed. You can also encourage them to self-soothe with a favorite blanket or stuffed toy.

- To help ease the often bumpy emotional transition process for foster infants and toddlers, use positive parenting strategies such as reading together, sticking with regular routines, and providing gentle, firm, and consistent discipline.

- Simple, direct communication with young children will ease their adaptation to your household. It is also helpful to model for children the healthy expression of feelings in words.

8

FOSTERING SCHOOL-AGE CHILDREN, 4–12

Foster children between the ages of 4 and 12, who attend preschool to middle school, are the subjects of this chapter. Like all school-age children, school-age foster children must contend with the usual rewards and challenges associated with attending school. But more than most, school-age foster children carry the extra emotional burden of not being sure what the future has in store for them.

Because of this uncertainty, foster parents who work with children in this age group must make a special point of being there for them. They are among the key adults in the lives of these children, and, as such, must be available to listen to them, reassure and comfort them, and provide them with emotional consistency and reliability at all times.

CHILD DEVELOPMENT IN EARLY SCHOOL YEARS

It's a good idea for foster parents to be aware of the benchmarks that denote routine development for young school-age children. Between the ages of 4 and 7, children are moving toward a greater command of logic and reason, becoming more social and less self-centered, and inclined to do more and more things independently.

Most children between the ages of 4 and 7 are actively working on the following developmental tasks:

- Figuring out how to differentiate between reality and fantasy.

- Becoming comfortable with their gender identities, their understanding of themselves as boys or girls.

- Understanding the similarities, differences, and relationships between their emotions, their thoughts, and their actions.

- Developing creative and effective problem-solving skills.

Child-development experts list the following indicators of potential developmental lag for children in the 4–7 age group:

- Being overly afraid, particularly of strangers, and experiencing an extreme form of separation anxiety when apart from their primary care providers.

- Excessive shyness and little to no interest in playing with other children.

- Bullying behavior.

- Problems with speech development.

- Bed-wetting issues and related problems, such as delayed toilet training.

Don't worry too much about isolated incidents. Any child might be shy on occasion or wet the bed once in a while. However, if a child in your care does not appear to be progressing overall, obtain professional advice.

CHILD DEVELOPMENT IN LATER SCHOOL YEARS

According to child-development experts, children between 7 and 12 take increasing pride in their ability to succeed at school, sports, and social endeavors. If their successes are few, they can suffer a loss of self-confidence and experience a sense of inferiority.

Most children between 7 and 12 are actively working on the following developmental tasks:

- Gaining greater physical strength and self-control.

- Learning and applying new skills.

- Interacting more with peers and getting more involved in competitive play.

- Forming personal values and a belief system that will start to shape their attitudes and behaviors for the rest of their lives.

For this age group, some of the primary signs of developmental lag include:

- Obsessing unhealthily about competition and academic performance.

- Rebelling excessively.

- Procrastinating with homework and other important tasks.

- Depending excessively on care providers for developmental tasks they ought to be able to do themselves, such as combing their hair or tying their shoes.

- Experiencing loneliness and social isolation.

- Developing inappropriate friendships with older children or teenagers.

- Stealing, lying excessively, or setting fires.

The more you know about the stages of child development, the more you can be of service to the foster children you are caring for.

It is essential for foster parents to keep caseworkers, pediatricians, and other care team members posted about worrisome or potentially worrisome behaviors a school-age foster child may be exhibiting. Often these behaviors can be curbed with the help of a child psychologist or another child-development professional—ideally one who specializes in the treatment of foster children with behavioral issues.

HELPING SCHOOL-AGE CHILDREN ADJUST

If school-age foster children in your care have been traumatized, abused, or neglected by their biological parents, your first concern will be to help them ease slowly and gently into your family's home life. They will be nervous, even scared, at first, so during the first few days and weeks of their placement in your home, focus on maintaining a quiet, peaceful environment. Try to use a soft, reassuring voice at all times. You want to let foster children know that they will always be secure and protected in your home.

You may want to state directly, and on more than one occasion, "We want you to know that you are safe here. In fact, your safety is our number-one concern. We became foster parents to provide safe, comfortable, peaceful homes for children just like you who need to live apart from their parents for a while."

BUILDING TRUST THROUGH "REPARENTING"

Caring for foster or adopted children who have been harmed in the past often necessitates a process known as "reparenting." Reparenting involves teaching traumatized children how to pick up the pieces of their shattered lives so that they can learn how to trust the adults now caring for them.

Reparenting will require patience, love, and compassion on your part. Hurt children may lash out at you in anger, not because they are feeling angry with *you*, but because they are angry at their biological parents and perhaps at the world as a whole. When they act out, they are displacing these feelings of hurt and anger onto you, because you are an easy target.

At first, it may be necessary for you to simply absorb some children's pain and anger, knowing that it is not in any way personal. Eventually, you will be able to help children in your care learn how to manage their anger, rather than allowing their anger to continue to manage them.

THE POWER OF POSITIVE EXPECTATIONS

Children in so much emotional turmoil may commit a dozen or more misdeeds in a day, and it may not be necessary to impose a consequence for each individual transgression. You may instead want to convey to your foster children that you have positive expectations of them and that you firmly believe they will ultimately succeed in getting their anger under control.

Virtually all parenting and attachment experts agree that it isn't helpful to respond to children's anger with anger of your own. After a child throws a tantrum, you will discover that a firm but caring tone of voice is more conducive to restoring peace and harmony than a voice raised in anger. In fact, getting angry will only compound the problem. Think of it this way: If two people raise the thermostat, the temperature in the room gets way too warm. Someone needs to turn down the heat.

It's not easy to foster hurt, traumatized children, but it can be profoundly rewarding. Children will become more trusting and less angry in a loving and safe environment where they understand that they can act out on occasion without fear of being severely punished. If you consistently respond to their anger and hurt with firm but gentle boundaries, the difficult behavior will decrease and, over time, the number of enjoyable days will increase.

DEMONSTRATING RELIABILITY AND CONSISTENCY

Two key factors in foster parenting success are reliability and consistency. These qualities let foster children know that you can be counted on to keep promises and follow through with plans.

For instance, perhaps you and a foster child in your care create a ritual: you go out for ice cream every Saturday afternoon to chat about the events of the past week. When you follow through on this plan each and every week, you reinforce the idea that you are dependable.

But let's say the child has a situation he wants to discuss with you that won't wait until Saturday. Making time to listen to the child and take what he says seriously when he needs you sends the message that you are reliable. You are a go-to resource whenever he needs help and advice.

SCHOOL ENROLLMENT

If you are caring for a school-age foster child, you may be responsible for enrolling the child in a school in your community. Enrolling a foster child in school does not have to be complicated, and there are ways to simplify the process.

WHAT IS THE PROCESS?

First, ask the child's caseworker about the procedure for a particular child and a particular school. Each school system has its own set of rules and enrollment paperwork, so the child's caseworker may not be familiar with the process at the public school in your area. If this is the situation, the caseworker may ask you to call your school's office directly and explain that you are a foster parent working with their agency and that you want to enroll a foster child at the school.

The school secretary or another staff person should be able to tell you the exact procedure for enrolling the child. Inform school staff that you will be filling out the necessary paperwork on the child's behalf, perhaps with the assistance of the child's caseworker. You may be asked (or you may ask) to go to the school in advance, perhaps with the child and the caseworker, for a pre-enrollment meeting.

PRE-ENROLLMENT MEETINGS

Pre-enrollment meetings can be useful all around, whether or not your own children are or were enrolled at the school. Visiting the school and meeting with some of the administrators might help reduce the anxiety of the foster children who are being confronted, yet again, with a new situation.

These meetings also provide an opportunity for foster parents to become acquainted early on with some of the key players at the school. Administrators and teachers often appreciate pre-enrollment as a way to get to know the children ahead of time, and to gather preliminary information about any specific educational requirements.

HELPING FOSTER CHILDREN SUCCEED IN SCHOOL

Home and school are the two central components of a school-age child's life. The latest research on how foster children fare in school indicates that foster children who receive academic assistance and emotional support from foster parents, teachers, caseworkers, and school administrators have a good chance of succeeding in school. And foster children who succeed in school often succeed in other key areas. They may develop enhanced social skills, for example, and make more friends. They may become more involved in activities outside of school and develop new interests. School, in other words—much like a caring foster family—can serve as a powerful stabilizing force in a foster child's life.

Yet there is no denying that foster children and youth face several specific educational challenges. For instance, if they drop out of school, they are less likely to earn GEDs than children who are not in foster care. In addition, studies show that foster children, as compared to other students, are often ...

- Absent from school more frequently.

- Less likely to read and perform other academic tasks at grade level.

- More likely to engage in inappropriate behaviors at school.
- Less likely to enroll in college upon graduation from high school.

Foster children in school must be given whatever support they need to succeed. They need to be accepted and integrated into the student body as would any other child. But they also need to be evaluated carefully in order to determine if they are getting the help and encouragement they require.

MAKING SCHOOL A TOP PRIORITY

Sometimes the caring adults who comprise a foster child's care team put so much emphasis on keeping the child safe and protected that, without intending to, they do not pay as much attention to the role of education in the child's life.

Of course, the safe and secure home lives of foster children are always of paramount concern. But school is a close second, because a good education is one of the surest ways to secure future success for any child. Therefore, anything that foster parents can say to foster children to emphasize the importance of a good education is beneficial.

Many foster children have their educational experiences interrupted frequently. Every time they are transferred to a new home, neighborhood, and school, they lose precious days of learning and fall behind in their schoolwork. They also lose social continuity and connection with children in their peer group. It is essential, therefore, that foster parents work with caseworkers and other care team members to enroll foster children in school as quickly as possible and try to keep them enrolled in the same school for as long as possible.

Foster parents have many requirements and obligations regarding the child welfare system. Often there are mandatory appointments with doctors, therapists, judges, lawyers, and other professionals. But every time foster children miss school for one of these meetings, they are missing out on lessons, homework assignments, and tests, causing them to fall behind. For this reason, experts suggest making such appointments after school hours as often as possible.

HAVING REASONABLE EXPECTATIONS

Ideally, foster parents should have reasonable and attainable—rather than excessively high or excessively low—expectations of the foster children in their care. Also, foster parents should be ready to adjust their expectations according to each individual child's needs and abilities.

Children listen to and heed the verbal and nonverbal cues of the adults in their lives, and they quickly become aware of what is expected of them at home, at school, and in other areas. If they sense that only passing grades are expected, they may perform to this level of expectation. If the possibility of college is never discussed, they may not feel that college is even an option for them. On the other hand, if foster parents consistently send foster children the message that they are bright and capable, even if they have special educational needs, the children will gradually internalize this message and start to believe that they are indeed bright and capable.

Keep in mind, however, that your enthusiasm, no matter how sincere, may take a while to register. Foster children may be suffering from anxiety, depression, and a variety of other emotional problems related to their past experiences at school. They may have already missed a lot of school, perhaps due to parental abuse and neglect, or perhaps because they have been caring for younger siblings. They may also be distracted by thoughts of their biological families, and by grieving for former friends, neighbors, teachers, and classmates.

However, many children, even those who have been traumatized, are emotionally resilient. In time, the positive feedback that they receive from you and other caring adults can help them believe in themselves and their abilities.

IT TAKES A VILLAGE: THE SCHOOL SYSTEM AND CHILD WELFARE

Foster parents have to deal with caseworkers and others in the child welfare system and with teachers and administrators in the school system. At times, the two systems may seem to have different missions and priorities. Child welfare workers are concerned first and foremost with the safety of foster children. Teachers and school administrators, on the other hand, focus on helping children develop academically and socially.

Of course, foster parents are required to work with representatives from both systems, which can be challenging. But if foster parents keep caseworkers informed of the children's progress at school and keep school staff informed of the children's progress at home, this clear communication can go a long way toward helping foster children succeed both at home and at school.

Foster parents are strongly encouraged to become as involved as possible in foster children's school events. You have doubtless heard the saying "It takes a village to raise a child." Well, it takes a lot of caring, concerned, involved adults to help a foster child succeed at school and at home. Foster children are more likely to succeed if all of the key adults in their lives work together as a team. You have heard the media talk about foster children who have fallen through the cracks of one system or another—the judicial, school, or child welfare systems—often because their care was mishandled or poorly coordinated. Teamwork is the best way to avoid such tragedies.

BECOMING INVOLVED

Become involved in the school lives of the children in your care. There are many practical things you can do:

- Meet with the foster child's teachers and administrators early in the school year.

- Explain to school staff (with the approval of the child's case-worker) that as long as the child is living with you, you will be responsible for signing all permission slips, report cards, and other paperwork, including approval to participate in sports and other school activities.

- Attend all parent-teacher conferences, and schedule extra parent-teacher conferences as needed.

- Pay close attention to report cards and comments from teachers on written assignments. If you have a question about a specific grade or comment, follow up by calling, e-mailing, or scheduling a meeting with the teacher.

- Consistently send foster children the following messages: school matters; homework is important; you enjoy helping them succeed in school; and education is the key to success as an adult.

Above all, keep the lines of communication open and continuous. Strong communication between foster parents and all those involved in the child's education is critical to academic success.

HELPING WITH HOMEWORK

Foster parents can also be very helpful in working with children as they tackle homework and studying. You should never complete homework assignments for a child (this sends the wrong message and doesn't help the child learn). However, there are many other ways to assist:

- Ask children about their homework on a daily basis. Be available to answer questions, help them make corrections, and proofread if necessary.

- Teach children how to break big assignments into smaller, less intimidating parts.

- Help children learn how to set priorities and goals.

- Create a peaceful homework setting that helps children study. The room should be quiet and uncluttered, with as few distractions (television, music, telephone) as possible.

- Make sure children have the tools they need: pens, pencils, paper, dictionaries, calculators, compasses, rulers, and, if possible, a computer.

- Set aside specific hours for doing homework. Children of all ages respond positively to routines, and this includes homework.

- Study time can provide an opportunity to teach values as well as academics. Remind all children in your care that it is never acceptable to cheat, to copy from others, or to ask parents, siblings, or friends to do their homework assignments for them.

- Instill a sense of accomplishment by praising children for finishing projects and meeting deadlines.

- When you're not directly assisting with homework, try to model positive homework behaviors by reading or working on something related to your job or household affairs while children are working on homework assignments.

- Reinforce memorization tricks that the children's teachers have taught them, and add some memorization tips of your own. Think about using rhymes to help young children memorize. And try creating flash cards for vocabulary words and basic math facts.

Celebrate academic successes and cheer children on for a job well done. At the same time, when it comes to academic setbacks and disappointments, don't spend too much time or energy on them. Focus instead on the principle of learning from mistakes and trying to do better next time.

In addition, don't focus exclusively on outcomes. Grades are not the only measure of progress. Effort is also important—perhaps even more so—

and should always be commended. If foster children have improved their grades from Ds to Cs and Bs since entering your home, tell them how proud you are of them. Your attention and positive feedback will mean the world.

EDUCATIONAL ADVOCACY

Many foster children have special educational needs. They may suffer from learning disabilities, developmental delays, speech and language impairments, ADHD, mental retardation, autism, emotional or behavioral issues, or visual or auditory impairment. Foster parents therefore often find themselves in the role of educational advocate, working with a child's teachers and school administrators to develop an educational program that is right for that child.

INDIVIDUALIZED EDUCATION PROGRAMS (IEPS)

In virtually all public schools in the United States, children with delayed skills are eligible for Individualized Education Programs (IEPs). The creation and implementation of such plans are free of charge. IEPs list the goals that foster parents, educators, and other care team members have for a particular child for the upcoming school year. They also outline the specific types of support and assistance the child must have to achieve these goals.

Frequently, children with IEPs can have their needs met in the same classroom as their peers. For instance, a teacher can work with a large group of students on one project while a reading specialist helps a smaller group of children with IEPs. As an alternative, or as a supplement, children with special educational needs may receive their instruction in a resource room outside of the regular classroom.

Sometimes, however, children's special educational needs cannot be met in a regular classroom or resource room. In such cases, the children may be sent to a special program designed for children with similar needs. These programs may be located at the school or at a different site. The teachers in these programs are specially trained and the class sizes are smaller.

Students are frequently referred for IEPs if their teachers notice that they are having difficulties with homework, tests, or class participation. A conference will be held with the child, the educators, the foster parents, and perhaps the child's caseworker as well, to determine the child's specific needs and develop an appropriate course of action.

Sometimes other specialists, such as a speech therapist, a special educator, an occupational therapist, a child psychologist, a guidance counselor, or others, may be asked to evaluate the child and provide input for the child's IEP. Some of the professionals who provide initial evaluations may also become a part of the child's ongoing IEP support system. For instance, children with speech impairments will often have weekly meetings with the school's speech therapist as part of their IEPs.

Based on the recommendations of this team of professionals, the educators and foster parents (and sometimes the caseworker) develop an IEP that includes short-term and long-term academic goals for the child. The IEP will be implemented throughout the academic year, with all the proper supports in place, to give the child the greatest chance at succeeding in school. If the biological parents are involved in the child's life, they may also be involved in the planning and implementation of the child's IEP.

REQUESTING TESTING

Teachers, biological parents, and foster parents can request testing and other educational services for children who are having academic difficulties. The results of the tests will help the teachers decide whether or not a child requires an IEP. The tests can also determine the specific educational services and programs that would most benefit the child.

Most of the time, foster parent–initiated requests for testing are granted without problems. As always, you can consult with the child's caseworker if you believe that the child's testing and other educational needs are not being adequately met and you are seeking ways to remedy this situation.

FOLLOWING UP

If a foster child in your care has special educational needs, you will want to follow up on a regular basis with the child's educators to make sure that these needs are being met. For instance, a child may have ADHD, a speech impairment, and a learning disability, and an IEP may have been developed to address each of these issues. Periodically, you will want to meet with the teacher and the other specialists on the child's educational team to check on the child's progress and to touch base about specific ways in which you can help.

ESTABLISHING SOCIAL NETWORKS

Academics are the main part of a child's school experience. However, not all important lessons are learned in the classroom. School is an ongoing opportunity to make friends and to join in recreational activities. So it is also important to encourage healthy social connections with schoolmates.

PLAY DATES

It's not unusual for children who get along well together in school to want to continue their relationship outside of school. If a foster child or a friend requests a play date, that is a sign that bonds are forming—and that's a positive development. However, do proceed with prudence where play dates are concerned.

Consult with the child's caseworker before setting up play dates. If your child has behavioral issues, there might be a concern about acting out in such situations. On the other hand, if your child is generally well behaved, you can build upon this strength by inviting a friend over after school. Also, note that all play dates with foster children and their friends must be supervised by an adult—preferably a foster parent—at all times.

If you or your caseworker have concerns about individual play dates, that does not mean your child cannot socialize. Some children fare better with organized and structured social activities, such as after-school sports or clubs.

EXTRACURRICULAR ACTIVITIES

Academics have to come first, but once foster children are acclimated to your home, their classrooms, and their teachers' expectations, you may want to encourage them to participate in extracurricular activities. These activities can help them become involved in the school community. They can also help them develop interests and hone skills.

On the other hand, some extracurricular activities, such as being part of a sports team or performing in a school play, can be time intensive. Participating in them can require sophisticated time-management skills from you *and* the child you care for. Think realistically about whether a foster child can participate in time-consuming extracurricular activities and carefully complete all of his or her homework assignments, too. Are the child's grades likely to suffer if he or she participates? As you make such decisions, remember that you can always discuss extracurricular activities with the child's caseworker and, if appropriate, the child's biological parents.

THE ROLE OF YOUR BIOLOGICAL CHILDREN

If your biological children spend time studying and doing their homework, they are already setting an excellent example for foster children. They are role models who set the standard.

Your older children may even want to function informally as tutors. Tutoring offers your children a chance to feel needed and useful, and at the same time benefits the foster child. Tutoring can also be a bonding experience for all of the children. Of course, you should always supervise foster children; tutoring sessions are no exceptions. Be certain that interactions are going smoothly. Make sure that the tutors are communicating accurate information in a helpful way and that those who are being tutored feel comfortable asking questions.

PTO/PTA PARTICIPATION

Foster parents are encouraged to take part in parent-teacher organization (PTO/PTA) meetings and activities if their busy schedules permit. PTO/PTA involvement is one of the most effective ways to stay in the loop with regard to school activities and functions. It also demonstrates to teachers and administrators that you are involved in the foster child's life and eager to contribute to the school community.

Today, many schools have websites that feature all kinds of useful information, including information about PTO/PTA events and opportunities to volunteer. Find out if your school has such a site, and if it does, visit it frequently. In addition to PTO/PTA information, you can sometimes learn about your children's pending assignments, field trips, extracurricular opportunities, and the like.

KEY CHAPTER CONCEPTS

- Developmental milestones for children between the ages of 4 and 12 revolve around increasing command of logic and reason, becoming more social and less self-centered, learning and using new skills, gaining more independence, and succeeding at endeavors like school and sports. If a child in your care shows signs of a developmental lag during these years, consult with a professional.

- Foster parents can help traumatized school-age children adjust at home and school by building trust and demonstrating their own reliability and consistency as care providers. The more children see that you follow through on your promises, the more they will trust and feel attached to you.

- You can simplify the school enrollment process by arranging for pre-enrollment meetings to discuss a child's needs and keeping the lines of communication open with children's educational teams. Communicating with the child's educators signals that you intend to be involved and supportive. In many instances, educators will enthusiastically include you in all discussions pertaining to the child's school life.

- When foster parents, child welfare workers, and educators work together to help children in foster care succeed in school, their teamwork can significantly improve foster children's academic performance and boost their self-esteem.

- Foster parents can facilitate the academic success of foster children by letting them know that school matters and that homework and studying are important. It's a good idea to model diligence and a love of reading and hard work and to speak often about the many long-term rewards of obtaining a good education.

- Foster parents should be aware of special education services such as testing services and Individualized Education Programs (IEPs). Foster parents ought to work closely with educators to create and carry out the IEPs of the children in their care.

- It is important for foster parents to help foster children by supporting them in establishing social networks with peers, arranging play dates when appropriate, and encouraging them to balance extracurricular activities with their academic needs.

9

FOSTERING TEENAGERS

Fostering teenagers brings many challenges, but also many joys. This chapter looks at some developmental milestones and challenges for adolescents ages 12 to 19, specific difficulties faced by teenagers in foster care, and permanency planning for teenagers in foster care. It also looks at some special circumstances, such as fostering pregnant teens and teenage mothers.

ADOLESCENT MILESTONES

As do babies, toddlers, and school-age children, teenagers have typical developmental milestones. During the course of their adolescence, teenagers between the ages of 12 and 19 are developing a sense of selfhood and identity based on evolving personal values and beliefs. They are understanding their roles in society and interactions with other people—including romantic relationships—as well as their particular interests and their dreams for the future.

Some chafing against authority during the teenage years is normal and natural, and some moodiness among adolescents is to be expected. But some teens have a great deal of difficulty negotiating this emotionally complex period in life and act out in ways that are damaging to themselves and extremely disturbing to those who care for them.

Signs that a teenager may be floundering on the road to responsible adulthood include …

- Chronic feelings of sadness, loneliness, and social isolation.

- Impulsive, rebellious, self-destructive behaviors, such as excessive lying, stealing, truancy, or running away from home.

- Repressing feelings or living in a fantasy world.

- Not bathing frequently enough or maintaining proper hygiene.

- Abusing substances such as alcohol, marijuana, or other illicit drugs.

- Developing an eating disorder, such as anorexia or bulimia.

- Engaging in promiscuous sexual behavior.

- Engaging in criminal or juvenile delinquent behaviors such as prostitution or burglary.

- Contemplating or attempting suicide.

In youth aged 15 to 19, a developmental lag may actually be expressed by a seeming desire to "grow up" and strike out on one's own by getting married early. Since early marriage is not a true path to emotional maturity, it often results in early divorce.

If a foster youth in your care exhibits any of the above signs of developmental lag, do not hesitate to bring these behaviors to the attention of the youth's caseworker. The caseworker will want to work with you and the rest of the youth's care team to develop an individualized treatment plan as quickly as possible. This plan will likely include one-on-one counseling with a qualified therapist.

SPECIFIC CHALLENGES OF FOSTERED ADOLESCENTS

Adolescence is a tumultuous time for everyone. In addition to pronounced hormonal shifts and bodily changes, teenagers are faced with new responsibilities and choices. Their expectations of themselves—and everyone else's expectations of them—are changing, seemingly overnight. Being a teenager in foster care can be even more challenging.

THE DESIRE TO BELONG TO A FAMILY

Teenagers in foster care want to feel that they belong somewhere and to someone. Many long to be a part of a family. Depending on their particular circumstances, some foster youth long to feel that they are part of both their biological family and their foster family.

Teenagers in your care may pose challenging questions in order to get a sense of your loyalty. For instance, they may want to know if you will always be in their lives. This longing for lifetime connections is perfectly natural. You will want to assure the teens in your care that their hopes and dreams are of great importance to you, that you are rooting for their current and future success, and that you plan to stay in touch with them.

At the same time, teenagers in foster care may also yearn to maintain strong connections with their biological families. Whenever appropriate, and with the assistance of their caseworkers, you should nurture this desire and facilitate meetings and positive connections between the teens and their biological parents.

THE DESIRE TO BUCK THE SYSTEM

Many teenagers go through a developmental phase during which they rebel against the adults in their lives. They are starting to develop their own opinions on a variety of topics, and some of their views may differ from those of their foster parents or their biological parents. Remember, a moderate amount of teenage rebellion and questioning of adult authority is simply a natural part of their journey toward identity and selfhood.

If a foster youth in your care is actively rebelling, it may be helpful to think back to your own adolescence. Perhaps when you were a teenager you occasionally rebelled against rules and regulations set by parents and teachers. These recollections can help you empathize with a foster teen who may be going through a defiant period.

Nevertheless, teenage rebellion can get out of control. It's one thing, for instance, for teenagers to announce that their musical tastes differ from those of everyone else in the household or that they have adopted a different political view. Indeed, such pronouncements can be viewed as a form of safe and healthy rebellion. Teenagers are in the process of developing their own tastes, opinions, and identities. Part of that process involves comparing and contrasting their new opinions with the opinions of others.

On the other hand, if a teenager's rebellious behavior begins to take a dangerous, self-destructive, or criminal form, such as shoplifting or engaging in unprotected sex, then you, the youth's caseworker, and a therapist must address this behavior immediately. Sometimes teenagers try to provoke you and the other adults in their lives in an effort to receive more attention.

Regardless of the youth's intentions, however, the sooner the care team develops an action plan, the better. If an acting out youth is not yet in therapy, this might be an appropriate time for him to begin one-on-one counseling. In conversations with therapists, foster teens may be able to immediately identify exactly what emotions they are experiencing (stress, grief, sadness, or anger) before they engage in certain self-destructive behaviors. Therapists can then help them identify healthier and more constructive ways to cope with these difficult feelings.

THE PUSH FOR AUTONOMY

All teens feel a drive toward independence, but this urge can be more complex in foster family situations. Extensive adult supervision is frequently a significant part of a foster youth's overall care and treatment. You may need to help teens balance their quest for autonomy and privacy with your ongoing responsibility to monitor and guide them.

You will want to encourage the foster teenagers in your care to be independent and to develop their own opinions and identities. At the same time, you want them to stay safe and learn how to use good judgment.

As cutting-edge brain-imaging research has shown, the parts of the brain responsible for making decisions are not yet fully formed in teenagers— and so not functioning at a mature level. The areas of the brain that are in charge of what scientists call "executive functions," such as planning for the future, controlling one's impulses, and exercising sound judgment and self-control continue to develop throughout the teenage years and even into the early twenties (with brain development often occurring earlier in girls than in boys). It is incumbent upon foster parents to provide teens in their households with nurturing guidance and support.

Ongoing supervision can be one of the best ways to steer teenagers toward good decision-making. After all, teens whose behavior is well monitored do not have as many opportunities to make poor choices. At the same time, there are various ways that foster parents can help the foster youth in their care become independent. Holding a part-time job for a few hours a week could be a constructive choice for some teens. A job can teach firsthand the values of reliability, teamwork, cooperation, and time management. (One caveat: academics must come first, and a part-time job may not be a good option for a teen who is struggling to keep up with schoolwork.)

ATTACHMENT ISSUES

Some teens in foster care may display an extreme tendency to distance themselves from their foster parents. This may be the result of early childhood trauma, the aftereffects of which may have been less noticeable at earlier stages of life. These unaddressed traumas can sometimes take center stage when a child becomes a teenager. In such cases, a teenager can display a form of attachment disorder, a psychological condition that interferes with emotional bonding.

Some teens with attachment disorder may seek affection indiscriminately from strangers or near-strangers. Others display antisocial behaviors such as bullying and emotional manipulation. Many such teens lack emotional authenticity and empathy. Often they struggle with impulse control and with paying attention. Sometimes they struggle with eating disorders.

If a teen in your care is evidencing signs of attachment disorder, it is time to seek help and support. Even in the teenage years, early damage can be repaired when the right components, including loving foster parents, empathic respite caregivers (as needed), and attachment-focused therapists, are in place. Attachment-focused therapy also helps teenagers understand and accept the fact that they are not to blame for their biological parents' abusive or neglectful behavior.

PERMANENCY PLANNING

The Adoption and Safe Families Act (1997) mandates that agencies and foster care teams devise and implement appropriate permanency plans for all foster children, including foster teens, in a timely manner. As with younger children in foster care, a permanency plan for a foster youth must be executed within a specific and reasonable time frame.

Permanency plans for teenagers in foster care vary from case to case. Often older foster youth have some say in their own permanency planning. In fact, some foster youth can identify key resources that care team members may have overlooked or not yet considered. By taking the ideas and preferences of foster teenagers into account, care team members acknowledge their respect for these maturing young people, which can boost the teens' self-esteem considerably.

Concurrent planning often plays a role in permanency planning for foster youth. For instance, the care team's initial plan may be to reunite a foster teen with her biological parents. However, if that plan is ruled out by a judge or by the foster care agency, a relative might be identified as an alternative permanent care provider or legal guardian. Concurrent planning ensures that there is always a Plan B.

In some cases, though not very often, foster teens ask judges to grant them legal emancipation. Depending upon the circumstances, such requests may be granted. A youth is considered legally emancipated when a court rules that he or she is officially liberated from the authority and control of another person, such as a parent.

TRANSITIONING INTO YOUNG ADULTHOOD

With permanency planning on the horizon, it is essential to do everything you can to help foster teens prepare for young adulthood. If not, they can fall through the cracks. For example, it is a sad fact that adolescents in foster care are less likely than their peers to graduate from high school. Anything you can do to prevent a teen in your care from dropping out of high school—or to encourage him or her to earn a GED if he or she has already dropped out—will be of great benefit to the teen in the future.

There are many other ways you can help foster teens in your care prepare for adulthood. You can encourage them to nurture the healthy relationships they form at this time of their lives—not only with peers, but with you and with other adults such as teachers, coaches, community leaders, and employers. Research shows that connecting with one or more caring adults can be an important factor in instilling young people with a sense of courage, strength, and conviction. These relationships can sustain them when they are contending with the challenges of young adulthood.

You can also help foster teens build up their reserves of emotional resilience. Be a role model and show them that life's setbacks and detours need not stop them in their tracks. Talk with them about the times you made mistakes or failed to achieve your goals at first and then rebounded—even benefited—from the life lesson you learned. The more you model resiliency and optimism, the greater the chance a foster teen will develop the necessary coping skills to navigate adulthood successfully.

HELPING FOSTER TEENS SOCIALIZE

As anyone who has ever been a teenager knows, socializing is an important dimension of teenage life. However, some teenagers in foster care do require extensive supervision, which can present certain challenges, both for the foster parents and for the teenagers.

FRIENDSHIPS AND PEER PRESSURE

All teenagers have a strong desire to fit in with their contemporaries. Foster teenagers might feel an even stronger need to fit in if they are struggling with difficult questions: "Is my birth family or my foster family my 'real' family?" "Is there a place in the world I can call my own?" It is essential to have continuing conversations with foster youth about the pitfalls of peer pressure. The more you talk honestly with foster teens about their struggles, the better equipped they will be to fight off negative peer pressure and resist giving in to peers who may encourage them to smoke, use alcohol or drugs, or engage in promiscuous behavior.

When it comes to drugs, don't tempt fate. Prescription drugs, and even certain nonprescription cough medicines, can be abused. Keep them in a locked medicine cabinet at all times.

You will want to encourage foster teenagers in your care to form and maintain healthy friendships. On the other hand, you do not want them to form bonds with peers who may not be good influences. So keep the lines of communication open and follow up on any opportunities to talk. If a teenager brings up concerns or questions about a particular friend, follow the teen's lead. Don't push too hard, but make a point of showing your interest.

Virtually all adolescent experts emphasize direct, honest, and respectful communication about these issues between parents or foster parents and teenagers. Here, in brief, are some of the most common suggestions:

- Avoid sounding critical or judgmental.

- Offer abundant support and praise for proactive behavior.

- Give the teenagers in your care personal space and privacy within reason.

- Maintain a sense of humor and a positive attitude.

One additional handy tip: parents and foster parents have observed that teenagers seem to open up to their parents when they have discussions in cars. Driving together, sitting side by side, not having to make continuous eye contact, can often lead to honest and revealing conversations.

DATING MATTERS

Dating can pose the same risks and benefits as friendships for teenagers, with one big difference: a sexual component. Dating involves learning how to take responsibility for one's sexual behavior. If a foster teen in your care is either dating casually or has entered a serious romantic relationship, you may need to discuss sensitive issues such as birth control and sexually transmitted diseases. If you have concerns about how to broach certain subjects, you can always discuss these issues with the teen's caseworker, or perhaps with his or her guidance counselor or health education teacher.

Entering a dating relationship with a caring boyfriend or girlfriend can be a positive experience for a foster teenager. Of course there is always the (fairly likely) possibility that the romance will come to an end, as teenagers can be fickle and inconsistent. If a breakup occurs, you will have to help the teenager cope with this disappointing turn of events. Be sensitive. Breaking up can be a blow to the ego as well as to the heart. Try to help your teen take the long view and, if you feel comfortable doing so, go ahead and share some of your own experiences about dating relationships that didn't work out.

Also remember that you and your partner are relationship role models for all of the children in your household. If you and your partner treat each other in a kind, supportive, respectful manner, the teenagers in your home are more likely to do the same in their dating relationships.

SEXUAL IDENTITY ISSUES

Some foster teens grapple with issues related to sexual identity and sexual orientation. Gay, lesbian, bisexual, and transgender (also known as GLBT) youth need a nurturing, accepting, nonjudgmental home environment. Unfortunately, many GLBT teens do not feel understood or accepted. GLBT teens are especially vulnerable to harassment by peers and by care providers. Not knowing where to turn, GLBT adolescents may run away from home because they feel safer on the streets. GLBT teens comprise nearly 40 percent of teenage runaways.

A disproportionate number of GLBT youth are in foster care. Those in foster care are more likely than other foster youth to be placed in group homes rather than in foster family homes. Sadly, however, many report being harassed and abused by other residents of these group homes.

If you have a teen who is GLBT, or questioning whether he or she may be, your support will be invaluable. If you believe you can provide such an environment for additional foster adolescents, please inform the caseworkers at your foster care agency. The need for caring foster parents for GLBT youth is urgent.

FOSTERING PREGNANT TEENS AND TEENAGE MOTHERS

Fostering teenage mothers is considered a specialty area within the foster care system. Pregnant teenagers and teenagers with infants are generally placed with experienced foster parents who have received special training. However, new foster parents often have questions about fostering pregnant teenagers and teenage mothers. If at some future time you consider fostering such young women, you should know there are many challenges associated with caring for pregnant teens and teenage mothers.

Young women who find themselves in this position often feel pressure to become adults overnight. They have to learn how to care for a dependent infant while still learning how to properly care for themselves. One component of a foster parent's job is to be a source of emotional support during these struggles.

PRENATAL CARE

If you are caring for a pregnant teen, you will probably be the one to drive her to her prenatal appointments at the obstetrician's office. But your responsibility for prenatal care does not end there.

A pregnant teen's doctor will tell her which prenatal services are essential. Your job is to make sure that she follows the doctor's instructions. If your foster teenager has any particular medical needs or issues during her pregnancy, you must make sure that she receives appropriate medical treatment. It is also your job to encourage her to engage in healthy, appropriate behaviors, such as regulating her diet and taking prenatal vitamins as directed by her doctor.

WHEN BABY ARRIVES

When the baby arrives, you must provide a safe, caring environment for the teenage mother and her baby, so that mother and baby can stay together. You must also help the teenage mother in your care learn how to be a parent. It is up to you to teach her how to care for a baby in a loving, nurturing way. She may be feeling overwhelmed, so help her stay calm, focused, and relaxed. Show her in words *and* deeds how to cope with this extremely challenging situation. Patience and compassion are both key to a successful outcome for mother and baby.

In addition, a teenage mother must learn how to prepare simple meals, do laundry, and live within the confines of a limited household budget. Be sure to model these household management skills. In addition, tell the young mother how much you enjoy teaching her these new household and parenting skills and how proud you are of her accomplishments.

Finally, be sure to closely monitor the medical and mental health needs of both mother and baby. Make sure that mother and child both go to all medical appointments, undergo any necessary medical treatments, and take any prescribed medications. Be sure to observe the young mother for any signs of postpartum depression (PPD). Symptoms of PPD include a sad affect; crying jags; sleep and appetite problems; lack of energy; anxiety; irritability; feelings of worthlessness or guilt; difficulty concentrating, focusing, or making decisions; and thinking excessively about death or suicide.

If a teenage mother in your care exhibits signs of postpartum depression, notify her caseworker immediately so that you can get her the appropriate medical and therapeutic treatment. It is also worth noting that while many teenage mothers fare well in a traditional foster home environment, others may do better in a therapeutic environment, such as a group home where the staff specializes in caring for teenage mothers and their babies.

SCHOOL SUPPORT FOR TEEN MOTHERS

Some public schools have excellent programs for pregnant teens and teenage mothers, with built-in supports already in place. The professionals who develop such programs understand that these teens are still children themselves. Their programs encourage these teenagers to stay in school rather than drop out.

Teenagers in these programs are required to take the same academic courses that their peers take, along with practical life skills courses designed to teach nutrition, health, parenting, budgeting, and managing a household. There may be a special health component where they will learn how to avoid getting pregnant again. The teachers may also prepare pregnant teens for the emotional and physical rigors of labor and delivery.

Some educational programs for pregnant teenagers and teenage mothers provide one-on-one counseling for program participants. Also, some schools provide babysitting or day care services so that young mothers can focus on their class work during the school day. If the public school in your area does not have an on-site program for pregnant teens and teenage mothers, the school administrator or the teenager's caseworker may be able to make arrangements for the teen to attend classes at a more appropriate school or program.

TRANSITIONING OUT OF FOSTER CARE

Every year, approximately 20,000 18-year-olds "graduate from" or "age out of" or "transition out of" the foster care system without having been adopted or reunited with their biological families. As you can imagine, this can be an extraordinarily challenging time for these young people.

Much of the data regarding former foster youth is alarming. According to studies, nearly half of the teens who transition out of care do not complete high school and only about 3 percent finish college.

In addition, former foster youth are more likely to suffer from mental illness and other health problems than young people who have never been in foster care. Many former foster youth report feeling isolated and cut off from their families and communities. A significant number get involved in criminal activity or end up living in poverty.

ACTING OUT AT THE TRANSITION

Before 18-year-olds transition out of foster care and start living independently, they may act out more than usual. This is likely because they are afraid of leaving your home, especially since they do not know what the future has in store for them.

You might want to think of a teen's pre-transitional acting out as a masking behavior or a show of false bravado used to cover up their underlying fears about going out in the world. So keep in mind that while a transitioning teenager's acting-out behaviors may be difficult to deal with, such behaviors are both typical and understandable.

FOSTER PARENTS' TRANSITIONING ROLE

When teenagers age out of the foster care system, their former foster parents are technically no longer responsible for them. In other words, foster parents do not have a formal or official role to play in a youth's transitioning process. However, foster parents can choose to be part of the "forever family" of the foster children formerly in their care.

Teenagers who once lived with you may be eager to stay in touch and seek your guidance and advice after they have transitioned out of the foster care system. Of course, only you can decide what role you want to play in the lives of these teens, but most foster care experts encourage these "forever" connections. The more support former foster youth have, the better their chances of succeeding in adulthood.

There are many practical tips that can help foster teens transition successfully into independent adulthood:

- Whenever possible, begin the transitioning process about a year before the teenagers move out.
- Teach the teens adult responsibilities, such as finding and keeping a job and saving a portion of the money they earn.
- Help them with apartment hunting, moving, and finding reasonably priced furniture, kitchen supplies, and the like.
- Offer to assist them with their job and college applications.

Above all, tell them you are proud of them and will continue to support them as they move into the world of young adulthood.

INDEPENDENT LIVING PROGRAMS

Policy makers, realizing the special challenges that former foster youth face, have been taking much-needed action to help these struggling young people. Two notable programs have been developed to assist former foster youth in transitioning successfully into the realm of autonomous adulthood. One is the John H. Chafee Foster Care Independence Program, created in 1999; the other is the Jim Casey Youth Opportunities Initiative, established in 2001.

These two relatively new programs can already point to some major accomplishments. For example, thanks to these initiatives, more than 200 former foster youth are now attending college in Kentucky, many of them faring well, both academically and socially. These promising figures indicate that, with just a modest amount of support and encouragement, former foster youth have the capacity to grow up to be self-sufficient, successful young adults.

For more information on the John H. Chafee Foster Care Independence Program, visit www.acf.hhs.gov/programs/cb/programs_fund/state_tribal/jh_chafee.htm.

For more information on the Jim Casey Youth Opportunities Initiative, visit www.jimcaseyyouth.org.

EDUCATION AND TRAINING PROGRAMS

Encouraging foster teens in your care to continue their education and training after they leave your home is an important part of the transitioning process. A number of educational and training programs for foster youth are already in place. Moreover, several states have tuition waivers for foster youth to attend in-state colleges.

One well-funded and well-publicized program is a component of the John H. Chafee Foster Care Independence Program. The Educational and Training Vouchers (ETV) Program was established in 2002. As the title of the program implies, it focuses specifically on the educational and vocational training needs of former foster youth, earmarking $60 million in federal payments to states for postsecondary educational and training vouchers. Each eligible young person can receive a voucher worth up to $5,000 per year to help cover the cost of education or vocational training.

By encouraging foster teens in your care to apply for programs like these *before* they leave your home, you are giving them a leg up in the transitioning process.

HEALTH INSURANCE FOR FORMER FOSTER YOUTH

Title IV-E ensures that all foster children up to the age of 18 are covered by Medicaid. The Foster Care Independence Act, passed in 1999, created opportunities for all fifty states to extend Medicaid coverage up to age 21 for foster youths who have transitioned out of the foster care system.

In 2007, the American Public Human Services Association published a report entitled "Medicaid Access for Youth Aging Out of Foster Care." According to this report, 17 states have enacted the "Chafee option" (a reference to the John H. Chafee Foster Care Independence Program) to provide Medicaid to former foster youth up to age 21. Presently, five more states are considering enacting the Chafee option. In addition, 28 states have found alternative ways to provide Medicaid to former foster youth: by categorizing them as "medically needy," by providing them with 1115 Waivers (also known as Medicaid Managed Care Waivers), or under other general assistance programs based on income. It is the hope of the National Foster Parent Association (NFPA) and other foster care advocates that all 50 states will enact the "Chafee option" soon, so that every former foster youth in the 18–21 age group will be covered by Medicaid.

KEY CHAPTER CONCEPTS

- Adolescent milestones include the formation of a personal sense of identity based on an evolving system of values and beliefs. Signs of developmental challenges include excessive moodiness or rebelliousness, poor hygiene, and lying, stealing, or running away from home.

- Foster teens often encounter special challenges. They may exhibit the symptoms of an attachment disorder, the seeds of which were probably planted when they were very young and were denied consistent loving, nurturing care.

- Teenagers in foster care are often more involved than younger children in their own permanency planning. Foster parents, caseworkers, and other care team members are strongly encouraged to take teenagers' opinions into account during the permanency planning process.

- It is important to help adolescents in foster care socialize appropriately with friends and dating partners and avoid the dangers of peer pressure.

- Helping adolescent girls become responsible mothers is the special task of those who foster pregnant teenagers and teenage mothers. Foster parents are advised to model good parenting techniques and to provide practical tips on topics like meal planning and household budgeting.

- Many hurdles are encountered by foster youth as they transition out of the foster care system, but foster parents can play a positive role in the transitioning process, choosing to become part of a young person's "forever family" even though they are not obligated to do so from a legal standpoint.

10

FOSTERING SIBLING GROUPS

Children between the ages of 11 and 16, teenage mothers, and sibling groups are the three populations now most in need of foster care. Sibling groups, including the importance of the sibling bond, special circumstances when siblings should be separated, and specifics about fostering sibling groups, are the subject of this chapter.

For some sibling groups, kinship placements, such as those with grandparents or with an aunt and uncle, are an effective way to meet the needs of brothers and sisters and maintain a strong connection with the children's birth family. Many foster care agencies encourage their caseworkers to seek kinship care as a first-choice placement for sibling groups. When kinship care is not a viable option, however, placing siblings together in a single foster home is the most recommended alternative. The latest research demonstrates that siblings placed together in a single foster home have fewer emotional and behavioral problems than those who are placed apart.

At this point, policymakers in most states understand the significance of the sibling bond and work toward placing sibling groups in foster care together whenever appropriate and possible. Many states have specific policies regarding the placement of siblings in out-of-home care.

You may not feel you are ready to foster a sibling group for your first or second placement, but you may want to consider it once you have some fostering experience. The need is great, and experienced, committed foster parents can really make a difference.

WHY THE SIBLING BOND MATTERS

For many people, bonds with brothers or sisters can be the most enduring relationships of their lives. People have a bond with their siblings from early childhood onward. That bond predates their relationships with their oldest friends, their first classmates, their spouses, their children, and other important people in their lives. In addition, sibling relationships often endure after parents or other primary care providers pass away. Even when adult siblings become estranged from one another, they still have a lifelong connection that can resonate on a deep emotional level.

Researchers explain that the bond between siblings is critical to the siblings' emotional development and well-being. Any sense of connection to one's family and one's roots is beneficial, particularly for foster children. When siblings can be placed together in foster care, the sense of continuity they have with their former lives can serve as a wellspring of strength and resilience.

Current research indicates that placing siblings together in foster care generally leads to ...

- A greater sense of emotional stability.
- Fewer placement changes.
- Shorter periods in placement.
- Fewer emotional and behavioral problems.

The attachment siblings feel for one another can also enhance their ability to bond with new care providers and foster parents, because one healthy attachment can lead to another. And since siblings also have a shared history, they can support each other as they grieve their shared losses.

WHEN KEEPING SIBLINGS TOGETHER IS NOT RECOMMENDED

For all the potential benefits of keeping sibling groups intact, foster care experts concede that sibling separation is preferable in certain circumstances. When there has been a history of abuse or other problems between siblings, or when one sibling has become attached to a foster family he or she has lived with for a long time, uprooting a child from a stable, nurturing foster home to be reunited with a sibling could be traumatizing. Costs and benefits must always be carefully weighed.

Sibling separation might also be called for when a child with special needs is placed with a foster family that is not able to foster additional children—perhaps due to space, money, or time limitations. In such a case, the benefits of receiving necessary care in a familiar environment might outweigh the benefits of reuniting with sisters or brothers.

All this said, there are some situations in which people might *wrongly* assume siblings should be separated. While some may believe that siblings who have large age gaps between them might not need each other as much as siblings who are closer in age, the opposite may actually be true. Placing teenage and toddler siblings together, for instance, may help the teenager feel more connected to the foster family and the toddler feel extra safe and supported. Some might also assume that siblings who bicker, tease one another, or compete with one another ought not remain together. But some degree of sibling rivalry is typical in most families and is not reason to keep brothers and sisters apart in and of itself.

The benefits of keeping siblings together in foster care usually far outweigh the potential problems, especially when it comes to behavioral issues. In general, siblings placed in the same foster home are less likely to act out than those in separate foster homes. Indeed, in some cases where separated siblings have later been reunited in one foster home, behavioral improvements have been dramatic.

When it is not possible to place siblings together, sibling visits are recommended. Assuming sibling contact is considered safe and healthy, siblings are also encouraged to stay in touch by calling one another and exchanging letters and e-mail messages.

SPECIALIZING IN FOSTERING SIBLINGS

There is a great demand for foster families who are willing to foster sibling groups. Unfortunately, it can be difficult for foster care agencies to find enough of these families. Even if a potential foster family wants to keep siblings together, space considerations can be problematic. Expenses can present another problem. The relatively low monthly reimbursements foster parents receive can make it difficult to care for more than one foster child at a time.

In addition, experts agree that sibling foster care can be hampered by an inefficient use of resources in the system. According to reporter Christopher Phillips, who wrote on the subject of sibling foster care in the January 1998 issue of *APA Online*, a publication of the American Psychological Association, "Even foster homes licensed to care for two or more children tend to be filled up piecemeal with foster children from several birth homes."

To read the *APA Online* article "Foster-care system struggles to keep siblings living together" in its entirety, visit www.apa.org/monitor/jan98/sibs.html.

Foster care agencies recognize that if they want to find families who can keep sibling groups together, they must provide adequate training and support. Many counties and states offer special in-service training sessions on fostering siblings. The trainers who run these sessions discuss the benefits—along with the challenges—of keeping siblings together. If you are interested in fostering sibling groups, be sure to ask your caseworker about these training sessions. You will also want to talk with fellow foster parents who have fostered sibling groups about their experiences.

ELIGIBILITY CRITERIA

The eligibility criteria to care for sibling groups vary from state to state and county to county. For instance, you may be required to have served as a foster parent for a certain amount of time before becoming eligible to foster sibling groups. You may also be required to participate in a specified number of in-service training hours on the subject of fostering siblings before becoming eligible. Ask your caseworker about specific requirements in your county and state.

MANAGING ADDITIONAL COSTS

If you are considering fostering a sibling group, it may be time to get proactive about your finances. Foster parents who want to foster sibling groups often find creative ways to manage their household budgets without depriving the children in their care. For example, they buy durable goods such as paper products in bulk and at discount stores. They may also wait for sales, clip coupons, shop for clothing at thrift stores, and make ample use of hand-me-down clothes, toys, books, sports equipment, computers, and the like.

Foster families also sometimes lend or exchange items with other foster families to reduce costs. This is a win-win situation for everyone. Talk to the foster parents in your support group about ways to make ends meet while caring for sibling groups. You should also be aware that some charity organizations provide items such as clothing, toys, bicycles, and school supplies to foster children.

There is an additional benefit to finding innovative ways to stretch a dollar. Without having to say a word, budget-conscious foster parents teach the foster children in their care how to manage money sensibly and responsibly. These are lessons that will serve them well when they reach adulthood.

SUPPORTIVE SERVICES AND ORGANIZATIONS

The availability of support for foster families of sibling groups varies from state to state and from county to county. The Neighbor to Family program is an example of an organization created to provide support for and meet the needs of sibling groups in foster care, their birth families, and the foster families who care for them. It was founded by Gordon Johnson, who is currently the organization's president and CEO. Prior to his involvement with Neighbor to Family, Johnson headed up the Illinois Department of Children and Family Services and served as president of Chicago's celebrated Jane Addams Hull House Association.

During his tenure with the Illinois Department of Children and Family Services, Johnson started to think seriously about the importance of the sibling bond for foster children. According to the Neighbor to Family website, www.neighbortofamily.org, "Johnson became convinced that the separation of siblings reduced the likelihood of reunification with parents, impaired a child's ability to bond with [foster or] adoptive parents, and increased the need for treatment of emotional and behavioral disorders."

In 1994, while seeking ways to keep foster siblings together, Johnson founded what he first called the Neighbor to Neighbor program. In 2000, he changed the name to the Neighbor to Family program. The organization encourages child welfare workers, birth parents, and foster families to support and sustain the sibling bonds of children in foster care.

The Neighbor to Family website lists the four key components of the organization's mission: placing foster children who are siblings together in a single home, keeping birth parents accountable for the well-being of their children, professionalizing the role of foster parents, and planning for permanency as a team effort. Children who are placed through the Neighbor to Family program are usually placed in close proximity to their birth families, hence the organization's name.

The Neighbor to Family program has expanded from Illinois to Florida, Georgia, Maryland, Virginia, and North Carolina, and is currently serving more than 2,000 children and families. If you live in one of these states, the organization is worth looking into. If you live outside the organization's scope, ask someone from your foster care agency, foster parent support group, or state foster parent association about similar resources in your area. Neighbor to Family works specifically with sibling groups. Foster parents should make their agency aware of the operational style of N to F so that families with siblings will benefit from that particular model.

KEY CHAPTER CONCEPTS

- Most states encourage foster care agencies to keep siblings together whenever possible and appropriate, as all relevant research indicates that this is usually the best arrangement for all involved.

- Kinship care can be an effective way to meet the needs of siblings and help them maintain a strong connection to their birth families. But when kinship care is not an option, placing siblings together in a single foster home is the recommended alternative.

- The bond between siblings can be critical to their emotional development and well-being. Placing siblings of all ages together in a single foster home can lead to improved emotional stability, fewer behavioral problems, fewer foster care placements, and significantly fewer days in placement.

- Foster care experts concede that there are a few circumstances in which placing siblings together in one foster home are inappropriate. This is true when there is sibling abuse or when one sibling—perhaps with special needs—is already firmly ensconced in a stable, beneficial situation.

- Foster care agencies are always seeking to train foster parents who are willing to foster sibling groups and have enough room in their homes to accommodate them. Inadequate financial reimbursement and an inefficient use of available resources often make it difficult to keep sibling groups together in foster care.

11

FOSTERING CHILDREN WITH SPECIAL NEEDS

Some children in foster care have special needs. This chapter addresses many of these needs, including the needs of medically fragile children, drug-exposed children, and children with fetal alcohol syndrome. The chapter also includes information about some of the more common mental health issues facing foster children, along with ways foster parents can help emotionally struggling children and youth get appropriate medical and therapeutic attention.

MEDICALLY FRAGILE CHILDREN

There is a great need for foster parents who are interested in caring for medically fragile children. A medically fragile child's physical condition, as documented by the child's pediatrician, may become unstable and change in an instant, triggering a life-threatening situation. Children with feeding tubes, respiratory tubes, shunts, tracheotomies, sleep apnea, severe diabetes, or other similar physical impairments are all considered medically fragile.

SPECIAL TRAINING FROM MEDICAL PROFESSIONALS

According to Judi K. Martin, a foster home certifier in Marion County, Oregon, foster parents who accept a child with a specialized medical condition will usually get equipment and training from a hospital. They will also get referrals for in-home assistance for specialized nursing procedures.

"In our county," says Martin, "we have a Department of Health Services (DHS) nurse who can train a foster parent in a specific procedure, but most of the time, the training comes from the doctor or hospital. DHS has funding for limited training, and we offer medically fragile training about twice a year. Foster parents often travel to other counties to get training as well."

It's important to note that foster parents can face several challenges when it comes to receiving comprehensive training. After basic training is completed, it may be hard to locate advanced or specialized training. It can also be difficult for foster parents to attend training, since it is hard to find appropriate respite care for medically fragile babies and children.

TIPS FOR CARING FOR MEDICALLY FRAGILE CHILDREN

Foster mother Amy Hardin found both joys and challenges in fostering (and later adopting) a medically fragile child:

> Our first child, Jon, was brought to us when he was 17 months old. He had many medical problems, which included being on a tracheotomy tube and having a hearing impairment. We fell in love with Jon the moment we saw him. I believe we needed to be able to care for him as much as he needed us. He had been left several times in the hospital alone and he was a very sad child. At the time we met him he was not eating and had no emotional connection with any individual. We trained for six days in order to bring him home.
>
> Jon made strides quickly and began walking about six months later. He has had a lot of challenges, and navigating the school system with a special-needs child has not been easy. He was

able to have his trach tube removed at age two, and we work with an ear, nose, and throat doctor at a children's hospital to help with his hearing impairment as well as with taking care of the trach area.

Jon is now eight years old and is in the first grade and is doing well. He will be receiving a BAHA implant—a surgically implantable system for the treatment of hearing loss—in the fall. He also has been diagnosed with ADHD and asthma, but overall, his health is good.

We did begin mental health therapy with Jon in the fall due to his not being able to show emotions. It was almost like he had none at all. He is doing well and loves his therapist.

I feel that it is very important to have the knowledge of what kinds of special needs your child has. For instance, our child has cognitive and comprehension issues due to hearing loss, premature birth, and neglect early on in his life. When I first heard the term "cognitive," I did not know exactly what it meant, so I asked over and over, and I researched. Never be afraid to ask for help. Jon was involved in "early intervention," a program in which someone comes to your home and works with the child until age three, and gives you ideas about how to help him achieve his goals. We have also worked with a physical therapist, and Jon currently is working with an occupational therapist to help with hand strength and writing.

Special-needs children are just that—they are very special. They look at the world with totally different eyes and they can teach you so much. We do have issues getting other children to play with him, and there are certain places that are very hard on children with special needs. You have to have an open mind and know the limits that a particular child has, but at the same time not place limits on them.

Hardin, who has fostered and adopted other children in addition to Jon, offers practical advice for caring for special-needs children:

- Be sure that you understand what the special needs are and that you educate yourself.

- A schedule is essential. Start with two items daily and then grow your list. Try a schedule with pictures to give children the independence and sense of mastery that they need.

- Schedule some "down time" every day. Whether it is for reading or playtime, just make it a period where the children have no expectations placed on them. This is a great stress relief, especially after school.

- Schedule time for yourself as well. Take care of yourself as a parent. Do little things like reading or watching your favorite television show.

- Listen to your children. They can reveal so much about what they need. When children have difficulty talking about things, give them crayons and a blank piece of paper. You will be surprised what they can say through art.

- Set goals, but remain flexible. Know that if a certain goal is not achieved, it is okay. There will be other goals and achievements.

- Don't dwell on things not done, but do celebrate the goals that have been achieved.

- Stay flexible. There are always good ideas to consider, and what may work for one child may not work for another.

- Be honest with your children.

Hardin also recommends making good nutrition a priority. Eating well is an essential factor in good health, and a varied, nutritious diet will provide energy not only to the children in your care, but also to you.

THE IMPACT ON YOUR FAMILY

Caring for medically fragile children can be extremely stressful for your entire family. The time and attention spent on foster children with special medical needs is time spent away from your partner and biological children. Therefore, if you are going to foster medically fragile children, incorporate your family in the child's care by assuming a "we're all in it together" attitude. Encourage and model time-management skills as well as patience and humor. Moreover, do not bite off more than you can chew: you can probably foster only one medically fragile child at a time.

Of course, fostering medically fragile children can be very rewarding. Doing so gives you a unique opportunity to model compassion and kindness for your biological children or the other foster children. Moreover, when your biological children spend time with a medically fragile child in their home, they learn about the enormous importance of helping others. These are life lessons that will stay with them forever.

CHILDREN EXPOSED TO DRUGS OR ALCOHOL IN THE WOMB

Children who have been exposed to drugs or alcohol in the womb present unique challenges. Many of them require foster care, as their parents continue to grapple with their own addictions and related problems. It is important, therefore, for new and potential foster parents to be able to recognize the symptoms exhibited by these children.

SYMPTOMS OF EXPOSURE

Children exposed to alcohol or drugs *in utero* are often of low birth weight, with a head that is smaller in circumference than average, and their physical development overall may be delayed. They may have birth defects, especially lung defects, and they may be more likely to test positive for hepatitis C or HIV/AIDS.

Other physical symptoms can include …

- Rapid breathing.

- Sweating and tremors.

- Increase in rigidity of muscle tone or lack of muscle tone.

- Excessive screaming and high-pitched cries.

- Abdominal pain and vomiting.

- Excessive yawning.

- Sleep problems, such as prolonged sleep, night terrors, and the tendency to awaken in a panic.

- Rapidly darting eyes (a condition known as nystagmus).

- Low tracking ability, or difficulty following a moving object with the eyes.

- Skin abrasions, especially skin breakdown on knees and elbows.

- Excessive nasal stuffiness.

- Vision and hearing problems.

- Increased skin sensitivity (and sometimes excessive diaper rash).

- Difficulty with sucking or swallowing (or frantic sucking) during feedings.

- Body temperature that often exceeds 99 degrees.

These children also often have emotional problems. Their inability to make eye contact, hypersensitivity, excessive fussiness, and proneness to tantrums can lead to difficulty bonding with caregivers. In addition, children exposed to alcohol or drugs may display a lack of boundaries and a disturbing fearlessness (including a lack of normal stranger anxiety). Conversely, they may have a tendency to be too quiet and seemingly too well behaved for their ages.

If a young drug-affected child in your care seems to be struggling with any of these symptoms, contact the child's caseworker or pediatrician for a referral to your local early intervention program. In some cases, for instance, when a drug-exposed child shows low or overly rigid muscle tone, physical therapy may be necessary. The foster child's pediatrician can make this determination and refer you to an appropriate physical therapist.

Consistency, stability, and routine are of enormous comfort to *all* children, and perhaps especially to those who have been exposed to alcohol or drugs in the womb. Make ample use of comfort objects, such as a child's favorite blanket or teddy bear, to help with times of anxiety and with any transition, such as when a child goes to bed, goes to visit biological parents, or goes to day care.

You may also want to try placing a struggling, fussy baby in a vibrating bed, seat, or swing. While not all young children are calmed by these devices, many find vibrating seats and beds very relaxing.

Finally, always talk to drug-exposed foster children in a low, soothing tone of voice, and when you sing and read to them, do so quietly and calmly. Try not to overstimulate them. Your primary goal is always to reduce their overall stress level.

TREATMENT PROGRAMS FOR DRUG-EXPOSED CHILDREN

Some states have created innovative programs to serve the specific medical needs of drug-exposed infants. The Pediatric Interim Care Center (PICC; www.picc.net) in Kent, Washington, is one such facility. The PICC Newborn Nursery provides specialized 24-hour care for drug-exposed and medically fragile newborns and brings babies safely through withdrawal from drugs, including heroin, cocaine, methamphetamines, methadone, and prescription drugs. The PICC program also facilitates visitation for families, provides caregiver training, follows the babies after they leave, and offers a range of community outreach and education services.

Your caseworker should be knowledgeable about the availability of programs like this one in your area. You can also research them yourself by using the Internet, by contacting hospitals, and by speaking with your child's pediatrician.

FETAL ALCOHOL SYNDROME

When mothers drink excessive amounts of alcohol during pregnancy, they often give birth to babies with fetal alcohol syndrome (FAS), a series of malformations and disabilities that only a doctor can officially diagnose. Many children with FAS end up in foster care.

A woman can give birth to a baby with fetal alcohol syndrome in two ways: by drinking heavily on a regular basis or by binge drinking periodically throughout her pregnancy. Everything consumed by a pregnant woman is also consumed by her unborn baby. However, a grown woman with a mature liver is able to metabolize, detoxify, and ultimately eliminate the alcohol from her system in a way that a small, still developing fetus cannot.

The only way a pregnant woman can be absolutely certain of preventing FAS is to abstain from alcohol completely during the full nine months of pregnancy. However, as long as pregnant women do not drink heavily on a regular basis or binge drink during pregnancy, their babies will not develop FAS. FAS is not a risk when a woman drinks only a small amount of alcohol once or twice during her pregnancy.

However, 44 percent of women who drink heavily and consistently during pregnancy will give birth to babies with FAS. The remaining 56 percent who engage in these drinking patterns might deliver babies with other alcohol-related problems, such as a milder version of FAS called fetal alcohol effects (FAE), a condition known as fetal alcohol exposed, or other minor to major developmental, learning, or behavioral problems. Very few will be entirely normal from a developmental perspective. Of course, other gestational factors play a role in an infant's health upon birth, such as genetics, the mother's eating habits, and the overall quality of her prenatal health care.

In addition to fetal alcohol syndrome, other possible outcomes of excessive drinking during pregnancy include an increased risk of miscarriage or stillbirth and babies born at low birth weight or length or with a small head circumference. There is also an increased risk of additional birth defects, more developmental delays, and lower IQ scores.

FAS can damage the central nervous system, which consists of the brain and spinal cord, causing mental retardation and severe learning disabilities. (In the United States, FAS is the leading cause of mental retardation.) Babies with FAS are usually born underweight, sometimes severely so, and their growth patterns are affected, so they continue to grow at a subnormal rate. The facial patterns associated with FAS include low-set ears, a flatness in the middle area of the face, a small head, a short nose, a thin upper lip, a small chin, widely set eyes, and a totally flat philtrum. The philtrum, also known as the infranasal depression, is a vertical groove in the upper lip located directly under the center of the nose. The normal formation of the philtrum is a key indicator of healthy embryonic development.

Additional cognitive, physical, and social problems associated with FAS are …

- Failure to thrive, or failure to eat and grow well.

- An overly pronounced startle response.

- Difficulties with sleeping.

- Problems concentrating and paying attention.

- Impulsive (and often self-sabotaging) behaviors.

- Excessive tantrum throwing.

- Struggles to socialize with peers.

- Difficulty mastering abstract thinking.

In older children, symptoms can also include stealing and excessive lying.

Any child can be born with FAS if his or her mother has used alcohol to excess during pregnancy. However, some groups are more afflicted by FAS than the general population. The incidence of FAS and FAE worldwide is 1.0 per 1,000 live births, whereas the incidence of FAS and FAE among Southwest Plains Indians is 9.8 per 1,000 live births. For genetic reasons, Southwest Plains Indians have a reduced amount of an enzyme needed to break down alcohol in the body. For this reason, women of Southwest Plains Indian heritage must be extra careful about alcohol consumption during pregnancy, ideally consuming no alcohol at all.

OTHER SPECIAL NEEDS

Children with other special needs, such as autism, Down syndrome, cerebral palsy, developmental disorders, and visual or hearing impairments may also require foster care. If you are interested in fostering children with special needs, tell the caseworkers at your foster care agency so that they can inform you about special training and other agency requirements.

MENTAL HEALTH ISSUES IN FOSTER CHILDREN AND TEENS

Many children in foster care struggle with mental health issues that can seriously impair their ability to function. You may be fostering a child or teenager who has already been diagnosed with one or more psychological or learning disorders, or a child or adolescent in your care may start to exhibit symptoms of a mental health problem. To prepare you for the latter possibility, this section describes symptoms of and treatments for some of the more common mental health problems that can afflict children and teenagers. These disorders include clinical depression; post-traumatic stress disorder (PTSD); attention deficit hyperactivity disorder (ADHD); attachment disorder (AD), which is also known as reactive attachment disorder (RAD); oppositional defiant disorder (ODD); and conduct disorder (CD).

CLINICAL DEPRESSION

Depression is radically different from ordinary sadness. Someone who feels sad once in a while is not depressed in the clinical sense. Everyone feels blue sometimes. But if a child or teen you are caring for feels sad nearly *all* of the time, and if that sadness is negatively affecting the child's thoughts, behavior, relationships with others, and school performance, he or she may be clinically depressed.

The following are the specific symptoms of depression:

- Feelings of sadness that do not go away
- Crying for no apparent reason
- Feelings of guilt and shame
- Reduced self-confidence
- A sense that life is meaningless
- A negative attitude
- A feeling of numbness, or a marked absence of any feeling at all
- A lack of focus
- Irritability
- Major changes in appetite or eating habits
- Disruptive changes in sleep patterns, such as insomnia or a desire to sleep all the time
- Chronic fatigue
- Excessive thoughts about death or about committing suicide

If a child or adolescent in your care appears to be experiencing several of the above symptoms, you should talk to the child's caseworker about getting the child into mental health treatment immediately.

The first thing a mental health professional will do is diagnose the type and degree of depression that a child is experiencing. There are different types of clinical depression, including (but not limited to) major depression, dysthymia (a milder form of depression), and bipolar disorder (also called manic-depression), which is marked by mood swings that go way up and way down. A psychologist can help determine which specific type of depression a child is experiencing, and can design an individualized treatment plan to meet the child's specific needs.

Fortunately, there are several effective treatment options for depression. Counseling, also known as psychotherapy or talk therapy, involves talking to a mental health professional, such as a psychologist, a school psychologist, a social worker, or a licensed mental health counselor. Therapists, particularly cognitive behavioral therapists, are trained to help young people change their thoughts and behaviors to start feeling better. They can teach children how to regain their sense of perspective and help them see the positive aspects of their lives.

The second treatment option involves psychotropic medication, or medication taken for the treatment of a mental health problem. Some children and youth respond positively to antidepressants, which treat depression by correcting a chemical imbalance in the brain.

While some depressed children and youth respond well to counseling alone or medication alone, many depressed children and adolescents respond best to counseling in conjunction with medication. Recent studies, however, indicate some risks associated with prescribing antidepressants to children and adolescents and they must be taken into account by the child's care team. Specifically, some children and teenagers have increased thoughts of suicide when they take certain antidepressants.

Most children and adolescents who enter treatment for clinical depression begin to feel better in just a few weeks. If a child or youth in your care is prescribed an antidepressant known to cause increased suicidal thinking in some young people, the prescribing doctor will closely monitor the situation. If there are problems, notify the doctor immediately so that the treatment plan can be modified.

Foster mother Amy Hardin writes, "Our oldest daughter in a sibling group that we initially fostered and ultimately adopted was discovered to have pediatric bipolar disorder, PTSD, and some other mental health issues. It has been tough at times … finding that out and trying to connect with her. Some days you do feel out of your league.

"We have a psychiatrist as well as a therapist for our daughter and for our family, and we have received a world of information. We have concerns, but have learned to enjoy today and try not to change tomorrow until we are faced with it.

"Our family has chosen to embrace the therapy and not run from it. It has been a huge help to my husband and me to know we don't have to know all the answers. It's okay to ask for help."

POST-TRAUMATIC STRESS DISORDER (PTSD)

PTSD is an anxiety disorder that develops after an individual has gone through one or more traumatic experiences. Many people think of PTSD as war-related, affecting mainly soldiers who have seen military combat. While military combat certainly is a common cause of PTSD, the disorder is not exclusive to combat veterans.

Many children who enter the foster care system have been traumatized, abused, or severely neglected. Not every child who experiences one or more traumas goes on to develop post-traumatic stress disorder, but some do. PTSD symptoms can also be found in children and adolescents who have witnessed abusive behavior. Children who have not been abused themselves but who have witnessed a parent or a sibling being made a victim of domestic violence sometimes experience PTSD.

The symptoms of PTSD vary, and some symptoms may be more prominent in some individuals than others. In addition, the symptoms can appear hours after the event or may take weeks, months, or even years to surface.

There are three different categories of PTSD symptoms: reliving the traumatic experience over and over again in one's mind; avoiding reminders of the experience; and hypervigilance or excessive anxiety. Sometimes a certain sight or scent or sound can trigger a PTSD flashback for a child or teenager.

Reliving the trauma can take several forms:

- Intrusive memories of the traumatic experiences
- Nightmares about the traumas
- Flashbacks so real that the victim feels he or she is experiencing the abuse all over again
- Feelings of stress and anxiety associated with reliving the trauma, including physiological symptoms, such as heart palpitations, excessive perspiration, tense muscles, rapid breathing, and nausea

Avoidance may cause the following symptoms:

- Avoiding or minimizing thoughts, feelings, places, people, and conversations related to past abuse
- Forgetting some or all aspects of the trauma itself
- Becoming emotionally numb, detached, and apathetic
- Losing interest in activities and in life in general

Children and teenagers who are hypervigilant or excessively anxious live in a chronic state of high alert. They experience some or all of the following symptoms:

- Problems falling asleep and staying asleep
- Chronic irritability and intermittent rages

- Difficulty focusing, paying attention, and concentrating

- Feeling the need to always have their guard up

- Jumpiness, or an exaggerated startle response

PTSD often manifests differently in younger children. Younger foster children with PTSD may exhibit the following symptoms:

- Wanting to be with you all the time

- Not wanting to separate from you to go to day care or preschool

- Regressing in such matters as potty training

- Having nightmares but not being able to describe the contents of their bad dreams

- Reenacting their traumas during playtime

- Drawing pictures or telling stories about their traumas

- Experiencing aches and pains with no apparent cause

- Behaving in an irritable and aggressive manner toward others at home and at school

If a child or teenager in your care displays any of these symptoms, you will want to contact the child's caseworker and care team immediately. They will help you find an appropriate counseling center for a mental health evaluation, and if necessary, follow-up treatment.

ATTENTION DEFICIT HYPERACTIVITY DISORDER (ADHD)

A significant number of children and teenagers in foster care are diagnosed with attention deficit hyperactivity disorder (ADHD). There are three main types of ADHD: the inattentive type, the hyperactive and impulsive type, and a combination of the two. Most children and teenagers with ADHD fall into the combination category. Because *all children display the following symptoms at one time or another,* only a pediatrician can officially diagnose a child or teenager with ADHD.

Please note that many of the symptoms of ADHD are also found in children with attachment disorder (AD). Indeed, there is some controversy over whether the behaviors exhibited by these children are due to attachment issues or if they are truly symptoms of ADHD. For this reason, it is essential for foster parents to work closely with children's pediatricians and mental health care providers to differentiate among these various possible diagnoses. Many of the symptoms are the same, and the current movement is to educate people on the differences, since it seems that kids in foster care are over-diagnosed with ADHD.

Children and teens diagnosed with the inattentive type of ADHD …

- Tend to ignore details and make careless mistakes while doing homework or other projects.
- Have difficulty sustaining attention while engaged in work or play tasks.
- Have problems with listening, even when addressed directly by a teacher or parent.
- Find it hard to follow through on instructions and finishing tasks.
- Have trouble keeping their thoughts organized.
- Tend to lose things frequently.
- Are forgetful.
- Can be easily distracted.

Children and teens diagnosed with the hyperactive type of ADHD …

- Tend to fidget and squirm a great deal.
- Have trouble staying seated even when parent or teacher reminds them to do so.

- Tend to run away and climb all over the place even when asked not to do so.

- Are not comfortable with or interested in quiet activities like reading time.

- Talk endlessly.

- Are always "on the go."

Children and teenagers diagnosed with the impulsive type of ADHD ...

- Cannot wait to take their turn, often pushing in front of other children.

- Interrupt others frequently.

- Act on impulse without thinking first.

Fortunately, ADHD is treatable. For some children, behavior modification therapy with a mental health professional is all that is needed. Others are helped by medications specially designed to treat ADHD. These now include nonstimulant medications, which are significantly less likely to be abused. Many children and adolescents with ADHD respond especially well to a combination of behavioral therapy and medication.

If you think that a foster child or teenager in your care may have ADHD, talk to the child's caseworker and make an appointment with the child's pediatrician for an evaluation. If the pediatrician diagnoses the child or teenager with ADHD, you will be advised about appropriate treatment options.

ATTACHMENT DISORDER (AD)

Attachment disorder is described at considerable length in Chapter 7 and Chapter 9. Briefly, children and youth who struggle with attachment and bonding problems often have a history of abuse, neglect, and abandonment, and sometimes of multiple placements with different families. Some children with attachment difficulties attempt to bond indiscriminately and inappropriately with people they have just met.

Older children and teens with attachment problems may engage in anti-social behaviors such as lying, stealing, manipulating, setting fires, and acting out in an aggressive and destructive manner. Children and teens struggling with attachment problems often make poor eye contact and seem to be lacking in genuine or authentic emotions, especially empathy. They may also have problems with learning and self-regulating, as well as issues with eating (such as hoarding food) and eliminating (such as wetting or soiling their pants or bed). They may show virtually no physical affection toward their primary caregivers or they may be excessively clingy. Whenever possible, children and teens diagnosed with attachment disorder should be treated by therapists who specialize in such problems.

OPPOSITIONAL DEFIANT DISORDER (ODD)

Children and teenagers with oppositional defiant disorder (ODD) are uncooperative, defiant, argumentative, and hostile, especially toward authority figures and care providers. They often have temper tantrums and refuse to comply with rules. They are irritable and angry much of the time and often purposely try to anger other people. When they get angry, they tend to make cruel, hurtful, insulting statements to their care providers and others. Most children and teens with ODD exhibit these negative behaviors at home, at school, and elsewhere, too. Often children with ODD also have ADHD or anxiety disorders or other mental health issues.

Many children and youth diagnosed with ODD respond well to positive parenting techniques, several of which are described in Chapter 7 of this book. For instance, foster parents of children and youth with ODD can reinforce the good behavior of these children by praising them enthusiastically when they behave kindly toward others or perform a task well. Counselors who understand ODD and approach therapy from a strengths perspective may have successful outcomes with these children. Sometimes medication is also recommended as part of a treatment plan for ODD.

CONDUCT DISORDER (CD)

Conduct disorder (CD) involves a complex set of emotional and behavioral problems in children and teenagers. Young people diagnosed with CD may …

- Display aggressive, cruel, and bullying behavior toward people and animals.

- Get into physical fights, sometimes with weapons.

- Lie, steal, or assault people sexually or physically.

- Have an almost uncontrollable urge to destroy property, often by setting fires or breaking and entering houses.

- Disobey rules, violate curfews, run away from home, and stop going to school.

Many children and adolescents diagnosed with CD have other mental health issues, such as a depressive or anxiety disorder, PTSD, or ADHD. Intensive (and often long-term) psychotherapy with a strong focus on behavior management can be helpful for these young people. Treatment may also include medication under the care of a psychiatrist.

WHEN INITIAL DIAGNOSIS IS INCORRECT

Diagnosing mental health disorders is often as much art as science. Consequently, a fair amount of trial and error can be involved. Sometimes a child may be incorrectly diagnosed at first, so the foster parents and medical care team need to do some detective work to figure out the correct diagnosis and treatment plan.

Foster mother Amy Hardin's daughter, for instance, was initially diagnosed with ADHD. However, right from the start, Hardin sensed that this diagnosis was incorrect, in large part because the child was not responding at all to her prescribed medication (a stimulant that, it turns out, was actually worsening her symptoms and increasing her anxiety).

By doing some of her own research and initiating a dialogue with her daughter's mental health care team, Hardin was able to convince the doctor and therapist to consider other possibilities. After an extensive re-evaluation of her symptoms, the doctors determined that she was suffering not from ADHD, but from pediatric bipolar disorder. Shortly thereafter, the medical team changed the child's medication and treatment plan accordingly. From that point forward, the child, though not completely out of the woods in terms of her ongoing mental health issues, was able to make significant strides nonetheless.

In a similar vein, another foster mother interviewed for this book— herself a developmental psychologist—recounted that while her son's school informed her that her child had ADHD and recommended Ritalin, she later ascertained that her own hunch was correct. Her son in fact had reactive attachment disorder. The symptoms of the two disorders, she noted, can easily be confused at first.

Many pediatricians and therapists who treat foster children and youth are very familiar with the attachment issues that afflict many children in foster care. This means that they understand that attachment issues must always be considered during a foster child's mental health evaluation, so that all the various types of attachment disorders can be ruled in or ruled out as possible diagnoses. Also, many doctors are willing to admit when an initial diagnosis (and accompanying treatment plan) was wrong. Of course, when a child's official diagnosis is changed, the treatment plan needs to be altered as well.

To be sure that a child is diagnosed correctly, be sure that he or she is carefully and thoroughly evaluated according to the procedures of *differential diagnosis.*

Differential diagnosis is the process a doctor uses to determine which of two (or more) diseases with similar symptoms a particular patient is suffering from. It is based on a thorough analysis of the patient's symptoms and all of the available clinical data.

KEY CHAPTER CONCEPTS

- There is a great need for foster parents who are interested in caring for medically fragile children and other children with special needs.

- If you choose to foster parent a medically fragile child, you will receive special training with regards to their condition and necessary interventions.

- Drug-exposed children and children with fetal alcohol syndrome often require foster care while their biological parents grapple with their addictions. Such children often experience physical challenges, developmental delays, and social difficulties.

- Many children and adolescents in foster care struggle with a variety of psychological and learning-related disorders. These include clinical depression, post-traumatic stress disorder, attention deficit hyperactivity disorder, attachment disorder, oppositional defiant disorder, and conduct disorder.

- Foster parents should contact a foster child's caseworker and seek appropriate mental health treatment if they believe a child in their care is suffering from any of these disorders.

12

COLLABORATING WITH BIRTH PARENTS

In the majority of foster care cases, the goal of permanency planning is to reunite foster children with their birth parents. This chapter explores the significance of the bond between birth parents and their children, the importance of repairing and reinforcing bonds between birth parents and foster children, the need for foster parents to treat birth parents as fellow care team members, the grieving process birth parents experience when separated from their children, practical tips to help foster parents work collaboratively with birth parents, and circumstances when family reunification is not an option.

THE BENEFITS OF BIRTH PARENT BONDS

Most children and adolescents in foster care want to stay connected to their birth parents and other members of their birth families during their time in foster care. If family reunification is the ultimate goal of a child's permanency plan, it is helpful if caseworkers explain clearly to birth parents the role of foster parents. Caseworkers should also emphasize to birth parents that if they fulfill all court-ordered requirements, their children's stays in foster care will be temporary.

Additionally, caseworkers should let foster parents know they should help the children in their care maintain a strong bond with their birth parents.

BIRTH PARENTS AS CARE TEAM MEMBERS

As a foster parent, you can facilitate the child-parent relationship in several ways. Caseworkers, birth parents, foster parents, and the child's legal representative (known as a court appointed special advocate/guardian *ad litem*, or a CASA/GAL) are all on the same team. Their shared goal is to provide children with nurturing care. It is important to work effectively and collaboratively with birth parents as much as it is to work well with anyone else on the team.

As Steve Baxter, an experienced foster parent and the co-facilitator of FPAWS, the Foster Parent Association of Washington State, says:

> If you are a foster family that gives a safe, loving home to a child for as long as the child needs a home, birth parents are very important for the success of your work. The best outcome for the child is usually to go home to a safe family. If you can help the child's parents create that safe family, you have done the best for that child.
>
> As a foster parent, I will never have the advantage the birth parents have through their attachment to their child. Even after years, the child's attachment to me will be like a thread compared to the attachment to the birth family.
>
> As foster parents, we must always speak as kindly to and as highly of birth parents and birth families as possible. Be truthful, of course. It is always truthful to say the family and parents love their child. Let the child know that you respect his or her parents and will work to keep their attachment intact. This is key to the child's self-worth and stability.
>
> Unless there are safety or legal issues, invite the parents to dinner with your family. It keeps the relationship intact and the parents get the experience of watching your family. You can mentor parents by letting them watch you. Invite birth parents to events and to holiday dinners.

EMPATHIZING WITH BIRTH PARENTS

It's fair to say that most birth parents who find themselves in the position of having to surrender custody of their children have not had easy lives. Many of them have grown up in poverty, have themselves been victims of abuse and neglect, or have themselves experienced foster care as children.

The more you remind yourself of these key facts when interacting with the birth parents of the children in your care, the more empathy and compassion you will bring to these interactions. Birth parents desire and deserve to be treated with dignity, humanity, compassion, and kindness.

Foster mother Amy Hardin writes of attending a meeting with the biological mother of a sibling group for whom she was caring:

> I was with the biological mother when she was told that the state was seeking termination of her parental rights. This woman was a broken person who had grown up in the foster care system herself and honestly just did not understand what having a child meant. At one point in the meeting I stopped the proceedings as things were getting heated and asked to just talk to the birth mother myself. I asked her how she planned on taking care of the children and she had no plan. She just wept and asked me if she gave them away would I take them. She could see that I loved them very much.

That moment represented a crucial turning point in the meeting. By addressing the birth mother with compassion and understanding, Hardin conveyed several messages at once: "I understand that you have been through a lot of pain in your life. I also realize that parenting is a difficult job and that right now you feel you are in over your head."

The birth mother could sense that Hardin and her husband were kind, nurturing people who would provide her children with a loving home and a good life. Knowing that, she asked if the Hardins would become her children's adoptive parents. Clearly, it was an emotionally

163

charged meeting. Yet, despite the fact that emotions were running high, Hardin's intervention enabled all involved to come up with an excellent permanency plan for the children.

Things will not always unfold this way, of course. The Hardins themselves have had other kinds of experiences. Amy Hardin explains, "There are some birth parents who do not want to meet us, and who honestly do not want to know anything about what is happening to their child while in our home. Remember, most of the time they are very angry; after all, their child is now living with us."

Nevertheless, Hardin believes that "It is very important to keep a link with birth parents if possible. Keeping school papers for them, or having their children draw pictures for them is a good way to keep the birth parents 'in the know' as to how their children are doing."

Hardin counsels foster parents to not do or say anything that might be perceived as judgmental toward the birth parents in front of the child. "Certainly," she says, "as a foster parent you will have feelings about these situations, but they are best expressed only to the caseworker."

Hardin also stresses the importance of ongoing communication and of family visitation time, the birth parents' time with their child. She says, "I have had phone calls at our home with birth parents and have met with them in their home when the time was right. We have fostered a child who was slowly reintroduced to her birth family's home, as she wanted to see where she would be living after leaving our care. We worked with the caseworker to make sure it was okay, and worked with the parents to figure out a good meeting time for them, and then we visited them. I believe the foster child needed to know that I would be okay with her going home."

When it comes to inviting birth parents to your own home, you will have to make the decision as to what is best for the child and your family. Some foster parents do not allow birth parents or other birth family members to come to their homes. They consider the foster home a "safe zone" for the child, and do not even give out information about where they live. But others feel differently. Some favor birth parent visits and believe that they provide an excellent opportunity for mentoring and role-modeling for birth parents. What's most important is for you to determine what works best for you and your family, perhaps making these decisions on a case-by-case basis.

HOW BIRTH PARENTS GRIEVE

Children are removed from their birth families when a judge rules that the children are not safe at home. The judge often tells the birth parents that if they participate in certain programs, their children will be returned to them. Upon first hearing the ruling, many birth parents begin to grieve. While no two people grieve in exactly the same way, research shows certain common threads.

THE FIRST STAGE: SHOCK

According to foster care experts, the first stage that grieving birth families go through is one of *shock*. During this initial phase, birth parents often beg caseworkers to give them another chance. They promise to take better care of their children. They cannot believe that the situation at home has become so bad that authorities have had to remove their children. Everything seems surreal to them, as if they are living in a nightmare.

At this stage, feelings of shock and sadness may be accompanied by anger and irrationality. In addition, many birth parents blame the foster care agency for the removal of their children, because it is too painful to acknowledge that their children are being removed as a direct consequence of their own behaviors.

THE SECOND STAGE: PROTEST

After the initial shock wears off, many birth parents enter the *protest* stage of the grieving process. This phase is characterized by physical symptoms, such as headaches, stomachaches, chronic fatigue, or insomnia. Out of anger, and to demonstrate their objection to the judge's ruling, birth parents in this stage may refuse to participate in court-ordered programs. For instance, if they have been ordered by the judge to attend parenting classes, they may refuse to do so because they believe that their participation would amount to an admission of guilt.

Birth parents might become quite inert and hopeless during this stage. They often feel helpless and fear that there is nothing they can do to get their children back.

THE THIRD STAGE: ADJUSTMENT

The third and final state of many birth parents' grieving process is called the *adjustment* stage. At this point, most birth parents have come to terms with the judge's ruling. While they may not like them, they have accepted the court-ordered tasks as part of their new reality. They have resumed their daily activities, are sleeping better, and feel more productive.

During this third stage, birth parents become receptive to the idea of working collaboratively with foster parents, courts, and caseworkers. Caseworkers and foster parents should respond positively to this interest in cooperation. For example, they might be able to help the birth parents focus on team unity, on doing what is best *for their children.* Also, they can help ensure that family meetings take place in a positive environment.

It is also important at this time for caseworkers to talk to birth parents about the precise role of foster parents in the child welfare system. Having this knowledge makes birth parents feel less threatened by foster parents. Also, by being included in the process, birth parents feel respected and valued.

Do note that the adjustment phase is an ongoing one. It takes time for birth parents to get a handle on how the foster care system works and to acclimate to living apart from their children. At times, they may feel depressed or upset because they know that their negative behaviors have resulted in the removal of their children. They may sometimes take these feelings of guilt and resentment out on you, the foster parent.

As time passes and birth parents get to know you better, they will realize that you want what they want: the best possible outcome for their children.

TIPS FOR WORKING WITH BIRTH PARENTS

Foster care experts and experienced foster parents offer some simple but important tips to help you in your team-building efforts.

CONTACT SOON AFTER PLACEMENT

If the child's caseworker gives you permission, get in touch with the birth parents as soon as possible after the child has been placed with you, ideally within two days. Making initial contact in a timely manner sends a message to the birth parents that you respect them and are thinking of them during this difficult time.

"JOIN WITH" BIRTH PARENTS

You may hear caseworkers and experienced foster parents talk about "joining with" birth parents. They are referring to including birth parents in the parenting process. This is particularly important when reunification is the goal of the permanency plan. If the birth parents learn to trust you, they may eventually come to view you as an ally: a mentor, a role model, and a parenting partner.

The following are some ways to "join with" birth parents:

- Tell the birth parents that you understand how sad they must be about losing their children temporarily. Let them know that their children will be safe and protected in your care.

- Actively seek out the advice of birth parents. You can ask them about their children's favorite foods, books, toys, TV shows, and bedtime routines. You might ask for their suggestions on how to make their children's bedrooms in your house comfortable.

- Ask birth parents for the names of the important people in their children's lives, for example, relatives and friends.

The general idea is to create an atmosphere of alliance, rather than one of suspicion or competition. No matter the content of the communications you make with birth parents, the underlying intent should be: *We are all in this together. We all want the same thing—the well-being of your child.*

ESTABLISH PHONE CONTACT GUIDELINES

It is imperative to establish guidelines for telephone contact between birth parents and their children. In general it is a good idea for foster parents and birth parents to agree in advance on the best days and times for telephone calls.

In some circumstances, regular e-mail contact between children and their birth parents may be appropriate, with established guidelines. The same applies to text messaging.

As foster children begin to trust you, they may be eager to share their feelings about their communications with their birth parents. They may also open up with more and more stories about their lives at home. Stay open to these communications. These children need very much for someone to hear them.

ENGAGE IN POSITIVE CONVERSATIONS

Birth parents, foster parents, caseworkers, and other care team members are encouraged to speak positively about all of the adults who play a role in the lives of foster children. Moreover, the care team must make sure that the children understand that they are in no way to blame for their current situation.

There is no point in playing a blame game in any form. Nothing constructive will come of it. Optimism and a proactive stance are what yield beneficial results.

ENCOURAGE FAMILY VISITS

Family visits, when deemed safe and appropriate, should be thoughtfully planned in advance. Here are some suggestions for making family visits successful and pleasant for everyone:

- Before the visit, encourage the children in your care to draw a picture or make a card for their birth parents. This small gesture will bring enormous pleasure to the birth parents as well as the children.

- Choose friendly, welcoming environments, such as a park (weather permitting) or a family-friendly restaurant. If you are using family visitation rooms at a foster care agency, be sure to check them out for suitable ambience in advance.

- Birth parents enjoy giving, and their children enjoy receiving candy, baseball cards, and other small gifts during family visits. Be appreciative of these gifts. They are indicators that the parents are trying to make amends for past behaviors.

- Help the children prepare "life books," scrapbooks in words and pictures about their lives in foster care. Encourage them to bring the books to family meetings. Life books provide birth parents with a visual and tangible sense of what their children have been feeling and thinking in foster care. Remember to include pictures of the birth parents and other relatives. The pictures let the birth parents know that their children love and miss them.

Finally, remember that many birth parents feel so guilty and ashamed of their past behaviors that they find it difficult to face their children during family meetings. You can put them at ease by praising them for their positive efforts and encouraging them for the progress they are making.

EASING THE TRANSITION BACK HOME

Maintaining regular and appropriate contact between foster children and their birth parents is the surest way to help the children transition back to their birth families. Sometimes, however, the first attempt at reunification may not work out. When this happens, the child may be returned to your care until the birth parents correct the ongoing problem.

Foster and adoptive mother Amy Hardin says of such situations, "We have worked with children that have been in our home and have returned to their birth parents' home only to later return to our care. In those situations, we have actually formed a one-on-one relationship with the biological parents. That has been challenging, but well worth the effort. Of course your heart wants so much for the child to not have to face anything wrong again, but there needs to be healing before that child and parent can go forward and resume living together on a permanent basis."

REUNIFICATION PROBLEMS

Not all stories of reunification have happy endings. There are birth families who don't want to cooperate or are dangerous to their children and others. There are absent parents. There are children who don't want to reunite.

Nonetheless, even when the birth parents are not directly involved in the child's life, there are ways to help children gather information about their families and understand their situations. Time spent helping children fill in their lives' gaps through talking and creating a life book builds a stronger relationship between foster parents, social workers, and the children. In the end, the child wins.

WHEN FAMILY REUNIFICATION IS NOT AN OPTION

In certain circumstances, birth parents are not a part of their child's permanency planning process. Of course this is the case if a child's birth parents have died. It is sometimes the case if birth parents are incarcerated for long periods of time. It is also the case when birth parents' parental rights have been legally terminated.

The parental rights of birth parents may be terminated by a court for any number of reasons. For instance, a judge may order the birth parents to attend parenting classes or a substance abuse treatment program within a designated time frame. If the birth parents fail to comply with court orders, their parental rights may be terminated.

Finally, some birth parents will never be able to care for their children, perhaps due to a physical illness or disability. However, even when reunification is not the goal, family visits are recommended when appropriate. The relationship between birth parents and their children should always be encouraged and developed. In these particular situations, it is understood that the foster parents will continue to provide day-to-day care for the children until they are grown.

KEY CHAPTER CONCEPTS

- There are many benefits to maintaining strong bonds between foster children and their birth parents. It helps for foster parents to think of themselves as role models, allies, and mentors to the birth parents of the children in their care.

- It is important to treat birth parents respectfully and compassionately and to include them as members of the child's care team. When birth parents consistently receive the message that they are respected and their opinions are valued, they feel inspired to complete their court-ordered programs in order to regain custody of their children.

- Many birth parents experience a three-part grieving process when their children are removed. This process typically starts with shock, gradually shifts to protest, and ends with adjustment. During this final adjustment stage, many birth parents come to grips with the fact that they are living apart from their children as a direct result of their own negative behaviors and may start to work actively on improving their behaviors.

- Family reunification is not an option when the birth parents of children in your care are deceased, are serving long prison sentences, are unable to care for their children due to a physical illness or disability, or have had their parental rights terminated by a judge.

13

FOSTER CARE AND YOUR EXISTING FAMILY

Serving as a foster parent can affect your existing family in a variety of ways. This chapter focuses initially on the impact of foster care on your biological children. Other topics addressed include foster care as a co-parenting activity; basic safety precautions; educating your extended family about fostering; tips for taking the stress out of family vacations, holidays, and birthdays; and positive life lessons that can be learned from living with foster children.

BIOLOGICAL CHILDREN OF FOSTER PARENTS

Foster parents intend to provide children in need with a secure, nurturing home environment. But how does the decision to foster affect the biological children of that foster family? What is the foster care experience like from the perspective of the biological children of foster parents?

Biological children of foster parents often report having mixed feelings about sharing their homes and their parents' attention with foster children. They may sometimes resent feeling pushed aside or as if their own needs have become secondary to those of the foster children.

However, many biological children also report feeling emotionally invested in and connected to their foster siblings. This tends to be the case when the foster children's behavior is not extremely disruptive and when those children seem likely to remain connected to their foster families "forever" in one way or another.

MEETING BIOLOGICAL CHILDREN'S EMOTIONAL NEEDS

Caring for foster children should never come at the expense of your biological children. It is essential to be sensitive to the emotional needs, wishes, and achievements of your biological children. Touch base with them regularly and include them in all decisions affecting the family. Indeed, foster care experts contend that biological children always need to be included in a family's decision to become a foster family. Older biological children are often encouraged to attend preservice and in-service foster parent training sessions.

Your biological children must always feel they are a top priority in your life. Even when a foster child in your care is acting out, struggling with medical issues, or needs to be driven to multiple appointments, remember that your biological children need you, too.

Touching base with your biological children daily will allow you to keep track of how they are feeling and what they are thinking. It is important for them to know that they can talk to you in confidence about everything, including their feelings about being part of a foster family. Listen carefully to what your biological children have to say about sharing their home and their parents with foster children, whether their feedback is positive or negative.

Don't hesitate to ask your biological children directly and frequently about what they need from you in terms of time, attention, energy, and activities. If, for instance, they want some "alone time" with you, ask your partner to supervise your foster children so that you can spend quality time with your biological children.

FAMILY TEAMWORK

Simply by virtue of being in your household, your family members become part of your foster child's support team. Biological children want and deserve to be a part of the family decision-making processes that have to do with fostering. Family teamwork and collective decision-making go hand in hand. For example, a decision made collectively might concern shared family goals, such as the emotional health and well-being of all members of the household.

When you talk to your biological children about family teamwork, be sure to tell them how much you value their roles and their input. Remember, you are asking your biological children to share time and attention with the foster children in your home, so it always helps to express your appreciation for their patience and understanding. Sometimes, a simple "thank you" can go a long way toward making your biological children feel included and appreciated.

INDIVIDUAL TEMPERAMENTS OF BIOLOGICAL CHILDREN

It helps too, of course, to take into consideration the individual temperaments of your biological children. When you make significant changes such as adding a foster child to your household, you can expect different reactions from your biological children based on their personalities and temperaments. An easy-going child may adapt to new situations with little difficulty. On the other hand, a child who tends to be somewhat anxious or very dependent could experience spikes in anxiety.

This does not mean that the parents of biological children with minor anxiety issues should never consider fostering. Many children adapt well to new situations after some initial uneasiness, but parents do need to factor their biological children's emotional needs and temperaments into their decision-making.

THE CHALLENGING BEHAVIORS OF FOSTER CHILDREN

Biological children frequently mention the disruptive behaviors of some foster children as one of the aspects of fostering that they find most challenging. All children—biological, step, foster, and adoptive—desire and deserve a safe, secure home life. A foster child or adolescent in your home who acts out continuously or excessively can be upsetting for your biological children.

Assure your biological children that you are trying to teach the foster children more appropriate behaviors. Ask your biological children for their patience, because long-lasting behavioral changes do not happen overnight.

Occasionally, you may want to remind your biological children why you and your partner decided to become foster parents: to provide temporary care for children in need. Knowing this may help your biological children cope during challenging moments when foster children require extra time, energy, and attention.

COUNSELING FOR BIOLOGICAL CHILDREN

When you become a foster family, your biological children may meet and live with children who have been abused or neglected by their birth parents. This can create a powerful sense of *cognitive dissonance* for your biological children. Cognitive dissonance is commonly described as the tense feeling that arises when an individual attempts to hold two conflicting thoughts in mind at the same time.

In the context of foster care, the biological children of foster parents continually try to make sense out of two conflicting thoughts: that all parents are supposed to nurture and take care of their children and that not all parents do—in fact, some harm and neglect their children. This cognitive dissonance can cause some biological children to experience a heightened level of anxiety, which may last for just a short time, as long as the family provides foster care, or even longer.

In addition, as you know, foster children sometimes act out as a result of having been traumatized. In certain circumstances, such as lying, hitting, or sexual acting out, these behaviors can have a negative effect on the foster parents' biological children.

Your biological children's cognitive dissonance about why some children need out-of-home care and the disruptive behaviors of some foster children can be extremely upsetting. If you sense that your biological children are becoming more anxious, or if you have other concerns about their emotional and psychological well-being, do not hesitate to raise the possibility of psychological counseling.

ADULT BIOLOGICAL CHILDREN'S VARYING PERSPECTIVES

A survey of postings on a public Internet message board yield some very different views of growing up in a family with foster children. Some reveal families divided, with grown children recalling that they felt their parents were unavailable to them because of the emotional needs of foster children in their care, not to mention all of the time spent with social worker visits and other protocols. They write of strained family finances and the resentments they caused. Finally, they write about feeling guilty for being unhappy when everyone else was telling them how "lucky" they were to have such caring parents.

Other postings, however, reveal families united rather than divided. Grown children write that while sharing their homes with foster children was not always easy, the love and tolerance in their hearts expanded over time. They felt proud of their parents for helping kids who had been mistreated in the past—and did not feel neglected as a result. They always felt included and cherished.

Could the parents described in the "families divided" have done things differently? It might have helped if they had ...

- Acknowledged to their biological children that they knew how difficult it was for them to share their parents with other children.

- Spent more time answering questions from their biological children and speaking directly to them about family teamwork.

- Invited their biological children to participate more in key family decisions.

- Opted for open, honest, give-and-take communication to explain how foster care works.

- Expressed appreciation for the willingness of their biological children to accommodate meetings with the foster child's care team.

- Spoken more openly and honestly with their biological children about financial matters.

The key to helping your biological children cope with living with struggling foster children is open, honest communication. Express your appreciation to your biological children, reassure them that their feelings are valid and important, and tell them that you are always ready and willing to hear their concerns.

REASSURING YOUR EXTENDED FAMILY

Your parents or siblings may have anxieties or preconceived notions about foster care. Tell them you are happy to answer any questions they may have. If they express concern that your fostering might cut into the time you spend with your biological children, reassure them that your biological children will always be a top priority and that you and your partner have discussed ways to balance the needs of all of the children in your household.

COPARENTING FOSTER CHILDREN

Fostering children and teenagers is a 24/7 job. Both partners in a two-parent household must be enthusiastic about serving as foster parents. As part of your decision-making process, have many conversations about what being a foster family means for each of you and how it may affect your relationship with each other and with your biological children.

HOW TO BE A SUCCESSFUL FOSTER FAMILY

To be a successful two-parent foster family, you have to keep your relationship with your partner healthy and going strong:

- Make time for just the two of you as often as both of your busy schedules permit.

- Find ways to unwind separately and together. For instance, after all of the children have gone to bed, you and your partner might find it relaxing to talk about anything *except* parenting. Or perhaps one or both of you can relax by reading, gardening, knitting, watching television, or doing crossword puzzles.

- Try proven relaxation techniques such as running, meditation, or yoga to destress and regain your emotional equilibrium.

- Maintain a peaceful household. Make a point of trying not to argue in front of any of the children, biological or foster.

- Agree to present rules and other important information as a united front to all children living in your household. Functioning as a fully united couple is a significant part of successfully coparenting.

- Keep the lines of communication between the two of you open at all times.

- Take advantage of respite services that your foster care agency offers. Respite is one of the surest ways for foster families to avoid burning out, so use it regularly.

- Consider taking substantial breaks between placements, even if the foster care agency asks you to foster a new child.

Finally, think seriously about talking to a counselor either individually or as a couple if either or both of you are feeling overwhelmed by the challenges of fostering.

LOOKING AT YOUR RELATIONSHIP

If your relationship with your partner is faltering, it is probably not a good time to become a foster family. Work on resolving your own issues as a couple before adding more layers of stress to your household.

On a similar note, if you are already fostering, but the challenges of fostering are negatively impacting your relationship with your partner or with your biological children, the time may have come for your family to take a break from fostering.

SAFETY PRECAUTIONS

Being a successful foster family also means being a safe family. Safety precautions should include supervising the foster children in your care at all times and making a written safety plan.

PROVIDING 24/7 SUPERVISION

Foster parents can help foster children stay safe and out of trouble by providing adult supervision at all times. You can use supervision time to teach appropriate behaviors.

Have a supervision plan for after-school and predinner hours, when the foster children in your care and your biological children may all be at home together. Sometimes you and your partner will want to supervise as a parental team, and other times you will want to alternate to give each other breaks.

Post a schedule and agree ahead of time to request schedule changes with as much notice as possible. But remember, stuff happens! If your partner needs you to cover for him once in a while, do so and assume that he will do the same for you. The important thing is that one of you is monitoring the children.

A WRITTEN SAFETY PLAN

Foster care experts recommend that foster parents devise an official safety plan for the protection and security of everyone in their household. In particular, if a foster child acts out in anger or exhibits any kind of inappropriate sexual behavior, the foster parents should have a written safety plan that can be implemented quickly if necessary.

Your written safety plan should do the following things:

1. Define the specific problem as precisely as possible. For example, if a foster child has a history of hitting other children or harming animals when stressed or angry, this is the main problem to be addressed in your safety plan.

2. Specify exactly who has to be protected when the child acts out in this way. For example, write down that the foster child, the other children in the household, and the family pets must all be protected.

3. Try to determine exactly when the problem behavior occurs. When might the foster child's anxiety level trigger an episode of acting out? For example, is the triggering event anticipation of a visit with the child's biological family or the visit itself?

4. Decide on the exact nature of the plan and who will carry it out. For example, the plan might require the foster parents to be particularly vigilant during those problematic few days prior to and following the child's visits with the biological parents. In a two-parent fostering household, the plan can be carried out by both foster parents. For instance, when one foster parent is cooking dinner or is otherwise engaged, the other foster parent will step in to provide one-on-one supervision.

To supplement your personal safety plan, keep a list of crisis phone numbers handy. (Include the child's therapist on this list.) Report any safety-related problems to the child's caseworker, or to additional authorities, if warranted. If the child or youth has committed a crime against another person or has caused significant property damage, be prepared to call the police.

Bear in mind that a particular safety plan may have to be in place for the entire time that a particular child lives at your house. Alternatively, the child's behavior may improve so much over time that it is possible to modify the original safety plan to reflect the child's new level of cooperation. If the initial safety plan does not work, foster parents should be prepared to re-evaluate it and make any necessary changes.

ADDITIONAL SAFETY PRECAUTIONS

In addition to formulating your safety plan, experts suggest some additional safety precautions in your home. If a foster child has a history of running away, you may want to install an alarm on the child's bedroom door or window, as well as a house alarm system. Place locks high up on household doors that lead to the outside or to the basement, but never on the outside of bedroom doors to lock children in.

Fire safety is also always a concern. Keep all matches and lighters in a locked container that is inaccessible to the children in your care.

Remember, when foster children act out or have difficulty controlling their impulses, especially with respect to anger and inappropriate sexual behaviors, it is likely because they have been abused and neglected and they have not yet learned appropriate behaviors and boundaries. The longer they live with you and experience your nurturing parenting style, clear structure, and boundaries, and the more opportunities they have to learn your household rules and expectations, the more their behavior is likely to improve. Even when their behavior improves, however, it is still a good idea for you to keep a general (though perhaps somewhat modified) household safety plan in place as a precautionary measure.

FAMILY VACATIONS

In order to take children in foster care on family vacations, you must have the approval of their caseworker, especially if you plan to travel out of state. If the caseworker grants permission, family vacations can be an excellent bonding time for the entire family.

However, vacations with foster children can also be stressful. Foster children who have stopped acting out, for instance, may resume acting out while traveling because their routines have been disturbed. All children, perhaps especially foster children, find daily routines very soothing. Any interruption of these routines can have a negative effect on their day-to-day behavior.

To prepare for this possibility, tell all of the children in your household that while vacations are fun and relaxing, they also mark a departure from the routines and comforts of your home. Assure them, however, that you can create a new set of family routines while on vacation. For instance, if you discover a restaurant that you all like, you may want to get into the "vacation routine" of having breakfast there most mornings.

If for any reason a foster child has not been granted permission to travel with your family on vacation, you will have to make contingency plans with the agency to provide respite care for the child. For this reason, you should give caseworkers as much advance notice as possible about upcoming family trips.

PREPARING FOR HOLIDAYS

Many foster children are painfully aware that some of their behaviors are not always consistent with social norms. They are eager to learn proper conduct and good manners, and family holidays are a good place to begin. You and your partner can teach them the importance of saying "please" and "thank you" and using good table manners at large holiday gatherings. You may want to have a practice or "dress rehearsal" holiday dinner at your own home before any big event with extended family to help alleviate any anticipatory anxiety.

You should also prepare foster children for the possibility that some well-meaning relatives may ask probing questions. Remind your extended family members that specifics about the lives of foster children are confidential. Even so, in a well-intentioned effort to be polite or make conversation, they might ask questions that make foster children feel shy or uncomfortable. To prepare the foster children in your care for such a scenario, let them know that they can answer specific questions with general answers. Also, assure them that, as always, you are there to help.

For instance, a member of your extended family might ask a foster child living with you, "Why do you have to be in foster care?" The child can give a general response: "I have to live in a safe place right now." If your relative continues to ask probing questions, the child can answer simply: "I'd rather not talk about that." Remember, you can always step in on the child's behalf with a pleasant comment or a change of subject.

BIRTHDAY PARTIES AND GIFT-GIVING

Experts warn that holidays and birthdays can be a difficult time for foster children, a time when they miss their birth parents more than ever. To lift their spirits, foster parents should encourage foster children to talk about any good memories they may have of past holidays. For example, ask the foster children living with you to reminisce about the happy birthdays they spent with their birth parents. They may choose to talk about these memories, write about them, or draw them. Later on, they may also want to add these writings or drawings to their "life books" or scrapbooks.

A birthday visit with biological parents can be especially meaningful to foster children who have been seeing their birth parents regularly during their placement with you. At the same time, special occasions like birthdays may make them sad. After all, birthdays are yet another reminder that they are living apart from their biological parents. Tell your foster children that you understand their feelings and that it is a pleasure for you to work with their caseworker to facilitate these important family visits, especially birthday visits.

When it comes to giving birthday parties for foster children, it might be best to keep the occasion fun but simple. Do not invite too many guests. You must be able to supervise everyone safely, while making sure the foster child feels special. Some children enjoy being the center of attention, while other children prefer not to be in the spotlight. As you make your preparations, take into account each individual child's wishes and temperament. Keep the gift-giving simple as well. Reasonably priced and homemade gifts that have a personal meaning often bring the most joy.

LIFE LESSONS

Serving as a foster family can be extremely challenging for you, your partner, and your biological children. The benefits, however, are equally rewarding. It may be hard to quantify these benefits, but they are very real nonetheless.

Children often grow up with a narrow understanding of life because they have not been exposed to life circumstances outside of their own immediate environment. They assume that all children have had a safe, happy, and healthy childhood like theirs.

Children who grow up with foster siblings learn otherwise. They discover early on that not every child has had a loving home life. They also learn that their parents and others like them feel so strongly about helping children in need that they invite these children into their homes until a permanent safe place can be found for them. This can be a source of great pride for your biological children.

Who knows? Perhaps your children will be so inspired by your decision to foster that they will want to become foster parents when they grow up.

Living with foster siblings will not only expand your children's world-views, but it will also teach them how important it is to help others. Not many children and teenagers have the opportunity to learn important life lessons about empathy, tolerance, responsibility, and compassion firsthand. If you are a foster parent, your own children will.

KEY CHAPTER CONCEPTS

- Serving as a foster parent can affect your existing family in a variety of ways, both positive and negative. However, if you are prepared, you can make fostering a generally positive experience for all involved.

- Foster parents must be sensitive to the shifting needs of their biological children and to the fact that the behaviors of some foster children can disrupt the lives of their biological children.

- Maintaining open communication, frequently expressing your appreciation, and including your biological children in family decision-making are three effective ways to make your children feel cherished, respected, and valued.

- In two-parent households, fostering requires the enthusiasm of both partners. To stay healthy as a foster care coparenting team, find the time and space to relax and destress, both together and apart.

- Parenting foster children and teens is a full-time job that requires 24/7 supervision of the foster children and a written safety plan. Depending on a child's behavioral progress or setbacks, you may need to modify the safety plan several times throughout the placement.

- Make careful preparations so family vacations, holiday get-togethers with extended family, and birthday parties are not too stressful. For instance, when you take children you are fostering on family vacations, establish vacation routines that can temporarily take the place of comforting home routines.

14

WHEN A FOSTER CHILD LEAVES YOUR CARE

Foster children leave foster homes for many reasons, but, whenever they do, it can be difficult for foster parents to adjust. Transitioning from one living situation to another also puts a heavy emotional burden on foster children.

This chapter looks at the transition process and its potential pitfalls. It also examines strategies for making the hard work of parting a bit easier on everyone involved.

REASONS FOR LEAVING A PLACEMENT

Sometimes foster children may leave your care for reasons that have to do with them—perhaps happy reasons, like family reunification. Sometimes they will be leaving for reasons that have to do with you, such as a change in your life circumstances. Here is a look at some of the more common reasons a foster placement might end.

REUNIFICATION

In most cases, if the birth parents successfully complete their court-ordered programs and if the judge and foster care agency determine that they are fit to resume caring for their children, the children and birth parents will be reunited. When safe and appropriate, family reunification is usually the ultimate goal of foster care.

Any time a placement ends in family reunification, it means that the child's care team has been successful in achieving its primary goal. The knowledge that you have performed your fostering duties well and that a family has been successfully reunited, in large part because of your efforts, can often soften the inevitable emotional blow of the child's departure.

Where family reunification is the ultimate goal, foster parents should keep two key points in mind at all times:

- First, they need to prepare for the child's departure from the first day of placement.

- Second, depending on the age of the child and the circumstances, they may be able to maintain contact with the child even after the child leaves their care.

PLACEMENT WITH A RELATIVE

If a relative of a foster child steps forward to care for a child, a judge and foster care agency may decide to revise the permanency plan so that the child can leave your care and move to the relative's home. Permanent placement with a caring relative is considered a successful fostering outcome for many children. Sometimes just recognizing this important fact can help foster parents better cope with the difficult process of letting go.

ALTERNATIVE FOSTER PLACEMENTS

Sometimes, for a variety of reasons, you, the judge, or the child's case-worker and foster care agency might decide that maintaining a particular placement in your home is not in the best interests of the foster child or of your family. The child may be moved out of your home and placed in a different foster home or in a therapeutic group home.

Good-byes under these circumstances can be emotionally complicated. You will be sad that the child is leaving, but you might also feel guilty or confused because the placement did not work out. You may even feel relieved. Keep in mind that not all placements are successful in the long term, and work on preparing yourself to move on.

CHANGES IN YOUR FAMILY CIRCUMSTANCES

Like everyone else, foster parents are sometimes caught off guard by life's unexpected changes. For example, you may have to move out of state due to a job change, causing a foster placement to come to an end. Likewise, if you or someone else in your family falls ill, you may not be able to continue fostering, at least for the time being.

Keep in mind that abrupt placement endings are far from ideal. It is preferable for all involved to have time to say good-bye. Anything foster parents can do to prolong a foster child's transitioning process—even if only by a few days or a week—can be beneficial for everyone involved.

ADJUSTING TO A CHILD'S DEPARTURE

When the time comes for a foster child to leave your care, you will likely feel a mix of emotions. You might feel sadness about the loss of the child and happiness about a job well done. You might also experience guilt ("What could I have done differently?"), anxiety, relief, and hope for the child's future. The specific mix and intensity of your emotions might depend on the child's age and the circumstances of the child's departure. In some situations, you may find yourself wondering: "Should our home be the permanent placement for this child?"

No matter how challenging a foster child's behaviors may be, you will invariably become emotionally invested in and attached to each child that you foster, which is what makes the departure of each child so complicated. How can you make letting go easier? One way is to remind yourself that foster care is usually a temporary arrangement. After all, the goal of foster care is reunification with the biological family, or, if that is not possible, with an appropriate permanent care provider.

On a similar note, foster parents should bear in mind that they are "parenting professionals" who are doing an extremely important job. This attitude of professionalism will not prevent you from investing emotionally in each child, nor should it, but it can make the process of saying good-bye to transitioning foster children less upsetting.

THE POSITIVE SIDE: IT'S A GRADUATION!

When a foster child leaves your care, try to think of it as a "graduation" and a cause for celebration. You, the foster child, and everyone else on the child's care team have been working toward this day for the duration of the placement. Reaching this point means that all of you have achieved a shared goal.

The children you have fostered will take your love and lessons with them when they leave your home for the next stage of their lives. Long after they leave your care, they will remember that you encouraged them and listened to them when they wanted to talk. Your nurturing will certainly leave a lifelong impression on their psyches and spirits. Knowing that you have made such a positive difference in their lives may help allay your sorrow when they leave.

Foster mother Amy Hardin shares her thoughts about the difficulty of saying good-bye to foster children:

Saying good-bye is always hard on the foster parents, because of the fear that you have for your foster children. For children it can be extremely difficult, especially if there are other children in your home. They, too, may have feelings of disappointment, dread, and fear.

One thing we did was very successful. We had a celebration for a foster child leaving our home. We have four adopted [former foster] children and we had one foster child at the time, a 7-month-old. We had cake and balloons for all the children, and the older children made some artwork for the child who was leaving. I believe it gave them a way to be happy about the change that was going on in their lives.

As always, be honest with the children. One child that we fostered was adopted out of our home and that was tough to explain to all the other children living with us. The adoptive parents came to our home and met her for the first time and she did cry about leaving us. The child's adoptive parents were so excited that they came back every night until she went to their home for good. Looking back, I believe that was a good thing for all parties involved. It gave us the closure that we needed for our family and gave the child time to feel some bond with her adoptive parents without having to leave one home abruptly and go to another.

After this child was adopted, the adoptive parents requested that we come to their home. We went one time. The child seemed a little confused that we were there even though she was very small. At that point we decided that for some time it would be best to talk on the phone with the parents and send letters to each other. We have made a very good friendship with the adoptive parents, but at the same time, have tried to back off enough to give the child time to bond with her parents.

The one thing that I try to keep in my heart and mind during each individual "letting go" process is that a child was helped during a very crucial time in his or her life. That is what a foster parent is there for: to help children get their feet back under them and help them build confidence so that they can go on. It may not be the same, but their lives can still be great. It will take time, maybe even a long time, but when you see the children's progress, it is worth it! Definitely!

Continues

Continued

It does hurt to lose foster children, but know that several determining factors have to be in place for a child to be returned home. Social workers are working hard and seeing another side to the situation that you may not be seeing. It's okay to ask for a better understanding of what is going on with the child's birth parents' progress. Also, if you have any concerns about a child transitioning back home at a particular time, it is okay to voice your concerns to the caseworker, but not to the parent.

THE TOLL OF TRANSITIONS ON FOSTER CHILDREN

Most foster children enter your home in an active state of bereavement. They are grieving the loss of their birth parents, siblings, neighbors, neighborhoods, friends, schools, and classmates.

While living with you, however, just as you inevitably grow more attached to them, they grow more attached to you and your family. Even children with attachment problems can develop feelings of affection for those who care for them. Therefore, when the time comes for them to leave your home, they might feel confused and bewildered, especially if they have lived with your family for several months or a year or longer.

HELPING CHILDREN EXPRESS FEELINGS ABOUT LEAVING

The children in your care will have mixed emotions as they transition out of your household. They will be sad because they are leaving your home. At the same time, they will be excited about going to their next home, especially if it is their birth parents' home. Doubtless, their excitement will be tinged with anxiety and fear.

Adults are familiar—although not always comfortable—with ambivalent feelings. They know what it's like to experience different, even contradictory, feelings at the same time. For children, however, and especially for foster children, ambivalent feelings can be confusing and upsetting. How can they be sad, happy, excited, angry, resentful, confused, and hopeful all at once?

Let foster children know that you understand their mixed feelings about leaving your care. Tell them you realize that it can be very confusing to feel upbeat and enthusiastic one moment, and then sad and fearful the next. Explain to them that these contradictory feelings are to be expected and are a natural part of the transitioning process.

To a certain degree, and always in an age-appropriate manner, you can share your own mixed feelings with transitioning children. Of course, what and how much you reveal will depend on each child's temperament and ability to understand and be comforted by such information. It might help older children to know that you, too, feel happy and sad about their upcoming departures. You are happy, you might tell them, because their futures look so bright. Also, since you plan to stay in touch with them forever, there is no need to be downcast. On the other hand, you are sad because you have enjoyed having them live in your home, and you will miss your daily face-to-face contact with them.

When you open up about your feelings, you are letting children know that it is okay for them to have complicated feelings and to open up about them. It is always preferable for both children and adults to express feelings verbally. Keeping emotions bottled up inside can lead to acting out. So encourage foster children transitioning out of your care to tell you what they are thinking and feeling. You could be preventing a negative incident.

COMFORTING TRANSITIONING FOSTER CHILDREN

There are several ways to comfort children who will soon be leaving your care. Listen to their concerns and anxieties. Offer positive, hopeful words of support and encouragement. Perhaps the best way to comfort transitioning foster children is to assure them you plan to stay in touch with them. Of course, the child's caseworker and new care providers must consent to this.

These days, many caseworkers, judges, biological parents, and others involved in the foster care system encourage foster parents and foster children to stay in touch after the children have transitioned out of the foster parents' care. To quote foster mother Shirley Hedges, "A child can never have too much love."

The key is to follow through on these promises. If you tell a child, "I will give you a day to get settled in your new home and then I'll call you on your second day just to see how you're doing," don't let anything prevent you from making that call. Children who have left your care need to know that they remain priorities in your life. You worked hard to build up their feelings of trust and attachment. Each time you make a promise and follow through on that promise, you remind them that there are trustworthy adults in this world and you are (still) one of them.

These post-transition contacts with foster children are beneficial to the children, as well as comforting to you. They allow you to work through your own sadness, while enabling you to keep track of the children's continued progress and development.

Post-transition contacts and visits can also help the biological parents or other care providers. If everyone agrees, you can offer to visit with the children to provide some respite from time to time. If you cultivated a strong relationship with the birth parents throughout the placement, chances are they will not feel worried or threatened by your wish to stay in touch with their child. Having worked with you, they'll know that you have their child's best interests at heart. Allowing their child to continue seeing you can only be a win-win situation—for the child, for the parents, and for you.

DISCUSSING POSITIVE ASPECTS OF TRANSITIONS

As foster children prepare to leave your home, talk to them openly and often about the positive aspects of this big life change. For instance, if they are moving back home with their birth parents, remind them how often they talked about missing their parents. Also point out how hard their birth parents have worked to regain custody, having fulfilled all the necessary requirements.

Tell them repeatedly that you plan to stay in touch with them. Telephone them soon after they move to their new home. Say something like, "You know how you've been having visits with your mom and dad during the time that you've been living with us? Well, now you will be living with your parents, and having letters, phone calls, e-mails, and visits from us!" Foster parents and foster children find it comforting to know that they will remain in each other's lives, although in a different way.

ADDITIONAL TRANSITION FACTORS

Many factors can affect a foster child's transition out of your care. One of these is the child's age. Others are the duration of the child's stay with you, as well as the specific circumstances of the child's departure.

THE CHILD'S AGE

Experts say that, for the most part, foster children under the age of three do not understand what is happening during the transition from your home to another setting. Older children, however, often realize precisely what is happening and want to know specific details about the transition process. It is important for them to feel included in the process, so be prepared to answer their questions when appropriate. For instance, if the child's caseworker and the court have specific plans for the transition, you can talk to them about the relevant parts of these plans. Also keep them posted about changes to these plans.

THE DURATION OF PLACEMENT

The length of time that foster children have lived with you also affects the transition process. Naturally, a child that has lived with you for only a week or two will have an easier time saying good-bye than a child who has lived with you for several months, a year, or longer. Likewise, it may be more difficult for you, your partner, your biological children, and other foster children in your care to say good-bye to a child who has lived with your family for a long time.

Be sensitive to the nature of the bond you and the child share. With long-term placements, a significant amount of discussion about future plans, as well as talk about the happy times you have shared, are appropriate. But this does not mean, of course, that children who have been with you a short while should be given short shrift. Acknowledge the ways in which you have enriched each other's lives, even if only for a brief while, and make certain the child knows you wish him or her the very best.

SPECIFIC TRANSITION CIRCUMSTANCES

Children transition in and out of foster care for different reasons, some happier than others. The better the child's upcoming circumstances appear to be, the likelier that the transition will be a relatively positive event.

Certain circumstances, however, can make the transition more difficult. When foster children who have been reunited with their biological parents must return to foster care (perhaps to your home) following new incidents of abuse or neglect, it can complicate the letting-go process significantly.

Should this happen, your belief in the child's family reunification plan will certainly be shaken. For the sake of the child, continue to be upbeat. If the biological family is reunited again in the future, perhaps the biological parents will ask for the support and services they need to take better care of their child.

PAVING THE WAY TO A SMOOTH TRANSITION

As difficult as it can be for children to leave your care, there are some time-tested ways to ensure a relatively smooth transition. If you follow these steps, you will bolster the child's feelings of confidence about the future. You will also ease their sadness at the separation.

GIVE CHILDREN TIME TO ADJUST

If circumstances permit, it helps to give children in foster care at least a month to adjust to the idea of leaving your home. Ideally, foster children should never feel hurried by you, the courts, their caseworkers, or any other member of their care teams.

A gradual good-bye, while still difficult, is not as difficult as a sudden good-bye. An abrupt departure can be emotionally wrenching not only for the child leaving your care, but also for you, your partner, your biological children, and any other foster children in your care.

ARRANGE FOR PRE-TRANSITION VISITS

If you are fortunate enough to have a month or longer to help a foster child transition, foster care experts suggest arranging for the child to visit his or her next home. The next home might be with the child's biological parents, a relative, or another foster family, or in a therapeutic group home. Whichever it is, the children's caseworker must approve any pre-transition visits.

The caseworker will ask you to accompany the child for the first visit. You should stay for the entire time, which could be a full day or just a few hours. If these daytime meetings are successful, the children's caseworker might grant permission for an overnight visit in the new home. For this overnight trip, you will want to stay for a while, but not for the entire visit.

PREPARE FOR ACTING OUT BEHAVIORS

Foster care experts warn that transitioning foster children may revert to previous negative behaviors prior to leaving your home. These behaviors are often exhibited by older foster children, who may be especially fearful about the future and the unknown. These children may have been in your care for a long time and have grown attached to you and your family.

No matter the reason for acting out, be assured that children acting out in the face of transition are experiencing grief, loss, and stress in anticipation of their departures. As suggested earlier, encourage children and adolescents to talk about their feelings rather than act them out in negative ways.

MARK THE OCCASION

When children are leaving your care to return to their birth families, some foster care experts recommend that you invite the birth parents to a celebration to commemorate this important life event. Marking this significant transition with a celebration can accomplish several important goals: It shows foster children that caring for them has meant a great deal to you, that you are proud of them, and that you will miss them very much. It also lets them know that moving to the home of their birth parents signifies a new beginning that is a cause for festivity.

GIVE MEANINGFUL MEMENTOS

Perhaps the children in your care have made "life books" or scrapbooks filled with photographs, drawings, and writings about their cherished moments with you and your family. If so, when the time comes for these children to move on, present them with their completed life books. Whenever they want to remember their time with you, they can pull out their life books.

Similarly, items of special significance such as blankets, stuffed animals, games, and toys can provide great comfort to younger foster children as they leave your home. The objects they cherished most while in your care will help them build an emotional bridge during times of transition.

GRIEVING FOSTER PARENTS

Foster parents are in a difficult position. They are asked to care for struggling children and to invest in them emotionally, but usually on a temporary basis. When foster children leave their homes, they are expected to disengage emotionally for the benefit of the children. In the transitioning process, the very real grief of the foster parents is often overlooked.

HOW FOSTER CARE AGENCIES CAN HELP

Foster care agencies can help grieving foster parents by giving them some time to grieve after a placement comes to an end. More specifically, caseworkers should not place another child in the home immediately after the departure of a child.

If you are feeling sad about a child's departure, it may help to talk to caseworkers and other agency staff. Many of them understand that these transitions can be as painful for foster parents as they are for foster children. In some instances, social workers and other agency staff have received special training on the subject of foster parents' grief.

Also, some foster care agencies offer training sessions to help foster parents cope with their feelings of loss and separation after a foster child has left their home. These training sessions can be particularly healing and helpful if the child's departure is recent.

Continue to attend your foster parent support group. If you are in the habit of going to these meetings on a monthly basis, consider increasing the frequency of your visits during transitions.

OBSTACLES TO THE GRIEVING PROCESS

To continue to do a good job with each new child who enters their home, foster parents need time to work through their feelings of loss over the children who have transitioned out of their care. According to experienced foster parents and other fostering experts, the potential obstacles to healthy grieving can include the following:

- If a child who is leaving care has been a behavioral challenge throughout the placement, the foster parents might feel as much relief as sorrow. This emotional ambivalence can lead to feelings of guilt that may impede healthy grieving.

- If foster parents are too busy caring for the other foster and biological children in their home, they might not have the time to grieve for the departure of a foster child.

- If foster parents worry about being perceived as emotionally ill-equipped to handle the temporary nature of foster care, they might be afraid to express their grief too openly. They might wonder if agency workers or fellow foster parents view their sadness as weakness.

Additionally, individual temperaments can be an obstacle to healthy grieving. For example, some foster parents may feel a need to be perceived as strong and self-confident at all times. They feel compelled to put on a happy face even when they are in a state of emotional turmoil. Foster parents with these attitudes may never allow themselves to fully experience their own deep sadness and sorrow when the foster children they have bonded with leave their care.

COPING STRATEGIES FOR GRIEVING FOSTER PARENTS

When a foster child leaves your care, remember that grieving is a healing process. Try to give yourself permission to feel all of your feelings. You will move through transitional times more smoothly if you don't try to suppress your natural emotions.

Try to find a brief period when you can be completely alone with your feelings, even if it is only a 10-minute shower. Use this time to cry if you need to. Really let your sadness out. Crying can be enormously cathartic and therapeutic. Since other people cannot hear you crying over the running shower water, you do not have to worry about upsetting the other children in your household.

If you are feeling stressed as well as sad, try different relaxation techniques, such as meditation, yoga, or exercise. If possible, increase these activities before and after a foster child transitions out of your home.

Finally, talk to experienced foster parents about your feelings of loss and sadness. Ask them for tips about how they handle their own grieving.

POST-TRANSITION CHALLENGES

Prospective and new foster parents frequently ask about post-transition challenges. We've addressed some of the most typical questions here.

What should I do if I think a child has been removed from my care too soon?

If you think a foster care agency or a court has moved too quickly to send a child back to the home of the biological parents or to another setting, you have every right to raise your concerns with the child's caseworker. As the child's advocate, you can request an extension of the child's placement in your home.

The caseworker will certainly take your opinion into account. Caseworkers know that the foster parents charged with caring for a child will have the keenest sense of the child's overall progress and remaining issues. The caseworker will likely present your concerns to the judge or an agency supervisor.

Speaking up on the child's behalf does not guarantee that a judge's ruling or an agency's decision will be overturned. If the ruling is not changed, you may want to let the caseworker know that you are available to foster the child again if the new placement does not work out.

What should I do if the child's post-transition care providers try to prevent follow-up contact between me and the child?

If the child's post-transition care providers are reluctant to let you see or speak to a child formerly in your care, you and the child's caseworker can try to arrange a meeting with them. If they agree to meet or speak with you by phone, talk to them about the importance of relationship continuity in a child's life. Discuss the benefits of the child maintaining close connections with those who nurtured him or her in the past. Perhaps these conversations will lead to renewed contact between you and the child.

If the child has been reunified with his or her birth parents after transitioning out of your care, and if you, the child's caseworker, and the birth parents have had a history of working well together during the child's placement with you, the birth parents might be quite receptive to your remaining in the child's life. You could serve as an adult mentor for the child and a respite care provider for the biological parents.

What are my obligations if I suspect problems with the child's new living situation?

If you have legitimate grounds to suspect that a child's new living situation is not appropriate due to abuse or neglect, it is imperative to contact your local department of social services to report the situation. After placing your call, let the authorities handle the matter.

Inform the department representatives that you are a foster parent, that you have fostered the child in the past, that you have remained in contact with the child and the family, and that you have reason to believe there are problems. These are serious allegations, so be prepared to support your claims with facts and, if possible, written documentation. Also, be ready and willing to answer follow-up questions from the department representatives.

What should I do if a child in my care does not want to leave my home?

Sometimes foster children struggle before, during, and after a transition. The best ways to help them let go are to assure them that you will always remain in touch with them and to follow through on your promise.

THE NEXT PLACEMENT

Sadly, there is never a shortage of children in need of foster care. A new child is always waiting to be placed with a caring foster family like yours.

How soon after one foster child departs should you take in another? Only you can answer this question. Look within yourself and be totally honest. The length of time you need to grieve may vary from placement to placement. If possible, try not to impose a specific time frame on yourself, as this will only add unnecessary pressure.

As soon as you feel the timing is right for you and your family, call the foster care agency to let the staff know that you are ready for the next placement.

KEY CHAPTER CONCEPTS

- Foster children leave foster care for various reasons, such as reunification with their biological parents or placement with a relative.

- Foster parents frequently have mixed emotions when foster children transition out of their care. They often feel a combination of sadness over the child's imminent departure and excitement tinged with anxiety about the child's future, as well as some relief.

- Foster children often suffer emotionally when they leave one home for another. Each time foster children are moved, they are forced, once again, to grieve the loss of a familiar living situation and adjust to a new one.

- Foster parents can help transitioning foster children by staying in touch with them after they leave. Visiting with the new care providers before the child leaves your care is another way to ensure a smooth transition.

- The grieving experience of foster parents is unique. They invest emotions, time, and energy in struggling children, but are also expected to disengage emotionally when placements end. It's essential that foster parents acknowledge their feelings of grief and allow themselves to fully experience them to resolve them, move forward in their lives, and accept future placements.

- If you have concerns following a child's transition out of your care, share your concerns with the appropriate authorities and be prepared to support your claims with solid evidence.

15

ADOPTING CHILDREN AND ADOLESCENTS FROM FOSTER CARE

This chapter explores adopting children and teenagers from foster care, including the reasons why foster children become available for adoption and the benefits of adopting a child who has been in your care for some time. It discusses the specific steps foster parents must take to adopt children and adolescents from foster care as well as financial assistance programs for adoptive parents of former foster children with special needs.

The chapter also covers post-adoption considerations and concerns.

WHY FOSTER CHILDREN BECOME AVAILABLE FOR ADOPTION

The primary reason a child in foster care becomes available for adoption is the termination of the parental rights of both birth parents. In most cases, and if appropriate, permanency plans aim to reunite children in foster care with their birth parents. However, when reunification of the child and the child's birth parents is not possible, caseworkers usually explore the possibility of a permanent kinship placement or adoption by a relative of the child.

When none of these options is viable, a foster child may become available for adoption. At that point, the child's foster parents may step forward to express an interest in adopting the child.

ADVANTAGES OF ADOPTING A CHILD YOU'VE FOSTERED

There are several advantages to adopting a child you have been fostering for some time. To begin with, you are already familiar with the child's background, medical history, emotional history, and birth family. If the child has special needs, you know precisely what they are and how to help the child on a day-to-day basis.

On a similar note, you have probably been working with the school system to meet the child's educational needs. The child's IEP (Individualized Education Program) has already been designed and is being implemented. If the child is in therapy, you are acquainted with the child's counselor. As well, you know the child's pediatrician, dentist, and other health-care providers.

If you decide to adopt a child already in your care, you may have to complete a formal adoption application and go through the approval process. This sometimes lengthy process includes paperwork, a home evaluation, and training classes. As usual, the exact requirements vary somewhat from state to state, so ask the child's caseworker precisely what is required of you. Fortunately, while you wait for the adoption to be finalized, your life at home with the child can continue unchanged.

Some states, however, require concurrent planning. Under concurrent planning, the child's care team works on several different possible permanency plans simultaneously. One of these possible plans may be adoption of the child by you. If the child's care team ultimately determines that your adopting the child would be the best possible outcome, you will already have taken many of the necessary steps during the child's placement with you, thereby significantly shortening the adoption process.

At the end of the adoption process, your family will become the child's "forever" or "permanent" family. Usually, this is a source of great comfort and joy for newly adopted foster children. On the other hand, some children have ambivalent feelings about being adopted because they still miss and grieve for their birth parents. These mixed feelings may cause children to act out. Generally, however, episodes of acting out become less frequent and severe with time.

Foster and adoptive mother Amy Hardin has addressed various aspects of her fostering and adoption journey throughout this book. Here she talks about adopting four children from the foster care system:

I have adopted four children from foster care. Our first adoption was of a special-needs child. We had him in foster care for about 18 months before his birth parents' termination of parental rights was finalized. His was an extreme case in that we were told that he might not live and he would not attend school.

I would say caring for him was the hardest thing I could ever imagine, due to the illnesses he had. There were days when all we did was practice walking and rolling balls. Today, though, I am happy to say that he is thriving and loves life.

There was a lot of red tape in this case and you could fill up a book with what happened during the adoption process. But every child deserves the chance to have a happy life. That is our goal as foster and adoptive parents.

Continues

Continued

The other children that we adopted were a sibling group of three. Their ages were three, eighteen months, and newborn. They came into our care as foster children and the adoption was finalized within six months. The biological mother signed them over, and the biological father did not show up for visits. The parents served some jail time, and at times, they could not be located.

I talked with the biological mother one-on-one, and she had been shifted from one home to another in foster care before the age of 12. Her mother had died when she was 17, and I don't believe she was ever really taught how to mother a child. She wanted to love, but just did not have the emotional capacity to do so.

I was given as much history as could be obtained from the birth families of our adopted children, so that if anything happened I would have that information. If at all possible during the adoption process it is great to get that information about the family's medical history because of health issues that may arise with your adopted child.

In our state, during the adoption process, there is an appeal process that biological parents have, with a time period of, I believe, 14 days, during which they can appeal the termination of their parental rights. Neither one of our adoptions was appealed by the children's biological parents. Regarding the sibling group of three, their biological parents were no-shows at the hearing to terminate their parental rights.

It has not all been easy sailing. Our oldest daughter, the oldest of the sibling group, had some problems. We later found out that she had been diagnosed with post-traumatic stress disorder, trichotillomania (a hair-pulling disorder), and pediatric bipolar disorder. It has been hard, but worth it, to see her begin to grow and do well in school, socially, and at home. We work with a therapist and psychiatrist every month and they are on call to us as well. She has made tremendous strides and we look forward to her having a great life.

A support group is wonderful and we have a county Foster and Adoptive Parent Association. We also have a state association and we have something called Alabama Post Adoption Connections (APAC), which is a great resource. You can request literature and information and they will send it to you. There are resources out there for foster and adoptive parents, and the Internet is a good place to start to locate them. You can perform a statewide search as well as a county level search.

Foster and adoptive care is a journey where you are never sure what the end result will be. You have to be happy for today and try not to worry about tomorrow. It will come soon enough.

PERMANENT FOSTER CARE VERSUS ADOPTION

Under certain circumstances, a child or adolescent in foster care will live permanently (until reaching young adulthood) with a particular foster family, but will not be adopted by that family. Permanent foster care is frequently referred to by the acronym *APPLA*, which stands for Another Planned Permanent Living Arrangement.

The criteria for implementing the APPLA permanency option vary somewhat, but not extensively, from state to state. In general, APPLA can be implemented for any one or more of the following reasons:

- The child's care team has decided that reunification with the biological family, adoption, guardianship, or placement with a relative are not in the best interests of the child.

- The child is currently living in an appropriate and nurturing foster home and the care team recommends that the child continue to live there until reaching adulthood.

- The child has bonded strongly with the current foster parent and that foster parent can continue to meet the child's needs on a permanent basis until the child is grown.

- The child's birth parents are involved with the child's life but are unable to care for the child full-time due to chronic emotional or physical health problems.

SOME ADOPTION STATISTICS

September 30, 2006, was a "snapshot" day, on which many important foster care statistics were officially collected by the Administration for Children and Families (www.acf.hhs.gov/programs/cb/stats_research/afcars/tar/report14.htm). The researchers found that 59 percent of former foster children adopted that year were adopted by their nonrelated foster parents, while 26 percent were adopted by a relative. In other words, when foster children become available for adoption, they are adopted by their foster parents nearly 60 percent of the time.

Many foster children who become available for adoption are over the age of two, are children of color, or are siblings who hope to be adopted together. There is also an urgent need for potential adoptive parents for older children in foster care. And many of the foster children who become available for adoption have special needs in one or more categories, such as a physical or mental disability or behavioral problems.

BASIC ADOPTION REQUIREMENTS

Prospective adoptive parents of foster children may be single or married. If they are married, most states require them to have been married for at least two years. They may own or rent their homes as long as they meet the size and safety requirements for their state. The ages of prospective adoptive parents may vary from state to state, with 21 to 55 being the most common range.

Felony convictions, which can include drunk driving, domestic violence, and drug crimes, will disqualify a potential parent from adopting.

There are no racial or religious restrictions for adoptions. Interracial and interfaith adoptions are permissible.

STEPS TOWARD ADOPTING A CHILD FROM FOSTER CARE

The steps toward adopting a child from foster care are often similar to the steps you had to take to become a foster parent. They include orientation sessions, a home study, interviews, and an application process complete with background check.

The entire process can take two months, a year, or even longer, even if you are already fostering the child you hope to adopt. Patience and flexibility are essential.

ORIENTATION SESSIONS

Like potential and new foster parents, prospective adoptive parents of foster children are usually expected to attend orientation sessions. During these sessions, facilitators will describe the adoption rules and regulations in your state and county. They may also provide preliminary information about foster children currently available for adoption.

HOME STUDY

Unless concurrent planning is going on for a particular child already in your care, potential adoptive parents of foster children are generally required to have their homes inspected and certified by a foster care or adoption agency. You can engage a private agency to conduct the study, but if you go the private agency route, you need to make sure the agency has been approved by the state.

Many private adoption agencies have religious affiliations, such as Catholic Charities, Lutheran Social Services, and Jewish Family Service. Public agencies tend to conduct their home studies via state social services offices. In some states, you are allowed to see your completed home study, so you may want to ask for a copy just to make sure that it is accurate.

THE APPLICATION

In many ways, the application to adopt a foster child resembles the application you completed to become a foster parent. You will have to provide all of the names you have ever used; your current address; your date of birth and social security number; your home addresses and the names of your employers over the last five years; your driver's license number; the dates of all your marriages and divorces; the names and ages of your immediate family members; your insurance carriers (auto, home, life, and health) and the policy numbers; your financial assets and holdings (real estate, stocks and bonds, bank accounts, and so on); and information about your pets and their vaccination histories. Additional information may be requested, depending upon the specific requirements of your county and state.

BACKGROUND CHECK AND REFERENCES

When you applied to be a foster parent, you and your family members had to submit to a criminal background check and provide personal character references as well as references from past and present employers. These same procedures are required of prospective adoptive parents of children in foster care.

HOME INTERVIEW

In the same way that potential foster parents are interviewed in their homes, individuals seeking to adopt children from foster care are also interviewed at home. You may be asked to participate in several interviews over the course of a few months. As you know from fostering, interviewers assess your parenting style and evaluate the comfort level of your home for children.

PRE-ADOPTION CLASSES

Potential foster parents are required to attend preservice training classes. Similarly, potential adoptive parents of children in foster care may be required to attend pre-adoption courses. The specific classes vary from state to state. Examples of training programs followed in several states include PATH, or the Parents as Tender Healers program; MAPP, or the Model Approach to Partnerships in Parenting; and the Parent Resources for Information, Development, and Education (PRIDE) training program.

TERMINATION OF BIRTH PARENTS' PARENTAL RIGHTS

Before a foster child can be adopted, the parental rights of both of the child's biological parents must be terminated. The termination may be "voluntary," meaning that both parents have willingly given up their parental rights, or it may be "involuntary," usually due to a court ruling specifying parental abuse or neglect.

ADOPTION FINALIZATION

To finalize the adoption of a foster child, a judicial proceeding called a finalization hearing, during which the adoptive parents are given permanent legal custody of the child, must take place. These hearings generally occur six to twelve months after the child's placement in your home. You, the child, your lawyer, and the child's caseworker are all required to be in attendance.

Often, the adoptive parents and their newly adopted child are eager to celebrate the finalization of the adoption. Once again, experts suggest that parents follow their children's lead in this matter. Remember, some children are more low-key than others and may want a small celebration, whereas others may prefer a more elaborate event.

MAKING GOOD USE OF WAITING TIME

You might think that the overwhelming demand for adoptive parents would speed up the adoption process, but this is not the case. The adoption process consists of many steps that are necessary for the protection of adopted children. Additionally, the social workers who facilitate the adoptions of children from foster care are busy with large caseloads. For all of these reasons, adopting a child from foster care is almost never a speedy process.

Experts recommend that you use the time constructively. For instance, if you are planning to adopt a child with special needs you may want, in addition to fostering the child you plan to adopt, to provide respite care for adoptive parents of foster children with special needs. You can also use this waiting time to talk to other adoptive parents of foster children.

FINANCIAL ASSISTANCE FOR ADOPTIVE PARENTS

Adoptive parents of former foster children with special needs are often eligible for various forms of financial assistance. Check thoroughly to see what kinds of aid might be available to you and your family.

THE ADOPTION SUBSIDY

Since 1994, the North American Council on Adoptable Children (NACAC) has headed the national Adoption Subsidy Resource Center, which is funded primarily through the Dave Thomas Foundation for Adoption. Under Title IV-E guidelines, adoption subsidies are available for children with special needs. If you are interested in learning more about your state's adoption subsidy, guidelines for every state are available via this page on the main NACAC website: www.nacac.org/adoptionsubsidy/stateprofiles.html.

U.S. TAX CREDITS

The federal adoption tax credit for special-needs adoptions was finalized in 2007. Adoptive families can receive a federal tax credit without having to document expenses if they can demonstrate that their adopted child has special needs as stipulated by the Internal Revenue Service (IRS).

The IRS considers any children that are hard to place for adoption as having special needs. This includes older children; children of color; sibling groups; children with medical conditions; and children with physical, mental, or emotional illnesses or disorders. In tax year 2007, the tax credit was $11,390 per child.

Adoptive parents of former foster children must complete IRS Form 8839, the Qualified Adoption Expenses form, to receive the adoption subsidy. The instructions for completing Form 8839 are available on the IRS website: www.irs.gov/instructions/i8839.

ADOPTION ASSISTANCE

All states offer some form of financial adoption assistance. If you were already fostering your child prior to the adoption, the monthly adoption assistance figure is often based on what you received to foster the child.

Caring for children, especially children with special needs, can be extraordinarily expensive. To maximize the monthly stipend provided to adoptive parents of former foster children, foster care and adoption experts suggest that you …

- Keep journals of children's progress, with a particular focus on behavioral improvements and setbacks.

- Request regular written behavioral reports and updates from children's schools, health-care providers, and therapists.

- Keep a complete listing of all respite care costs incurred.

Accuracy is important. Review all adoption assistance paperwork carefully before signing.

MEDICAL ASSISTANCE

You may be eligible for medical assistance from your state. Medical assistance may cover some costs that your health insurance does not cover. Ask your child's adoption worker about medical assistance programs in your area.

SOCIAL SECURITY BENEFITS

Some children with special needs or specific mental or physical disabilities are eligible to receive monthly payments from the Social Security Insurance (SSI) program. For a child to qualify, you will need to complete a Child Disability Report (www.ssa.gov/applyfordisability/child.htm) on the child's behalf.

WOMEN, INFANTS, AND CHILDREN (WIC) PROGRAM

Many people are unaware that foster and adoptive parents of children with special needs are often eligible for WIC. The WIC program provides healthy food not only to low-income families, but also to any family receiving medical assistance from the government.

POST-ADOPTION CONSIDERATIONS

After you adopt a former foster child, post-adoption issues can arise. As always, it's prudent to be prepared.

UPDATING IMPORTANT DOCUMENTS

Update all of your insurance policies to reflect the addition of the adopted child to your household. It may also be necessary to make changes in the beneficiaries listed on your insurance policies and in your will.

POST-ADOPTION HOME VISITS

A representative from social services will visit your home from time to time following your adoption of a former foster child. They are not seeking to invade your privacy or judge your parenting abilities. Rather, they are there to answer your questions and check on the progress of your newly adopted child. They also want to make sure that you are receiving all of the support services you need.

USING ADOPTION SUPPORT GROUPS

Support groups for adoptive foster parents are an excellent source of comfort, hope, and emotional nourishment. The people who can best understand what you are going through are those individuals who have had similar experiences. Like you, they have contended with bureaucratic red tape, waited patiently for an adoption to be finalized, provided loving care to emotionally struggling children who had mixed feelings about being adopted, and so on. Turn to your fellow foster and adoptive parents for advice and comfort.

If you are seeking a local support group for adoptive parents, investigate the useful resources listed at www.adoptivefamilies.com/support_group. php. Your child's adoption worker, therapist, and school counselors are additional sources of information about local support groups for adoptive parents of former foster children.

ADOPTION MENTORS

A new adoptive parent may also want to seek out a mentor, perhaps a member of his or her adoption support group. A strong relationship with a wise mentor can provide new adoptive parents with the emotional life support they need to keep going when the going gets tough.

Children are not the only ones who need nurturing and tender loving care. Adults also need to know that they have supporters, people who are rooting for them and their children to succeed. Mentors understand how hard it can be to parent children who have been through so much in their young lives, and they are more than happy to share their own experiences and hard-earned wisdom with you.

FOSTERING AND ADOPTION WORKSHOPS AND SEMINARS

Foster and adoptive parents are extremely busy people, but many of them find that taking the time to attend a few educational seminars throughout the year can be both educational and emotionally restorative. In addition, foster parents who want to maintain their licensure are required to attend a certain number of in-service trainings each year.

The National Foster Parent Association (NFPA; www.nfpaonline.org) holds an annual training and support conference for foster parents. The NFPA website also regularly features information about various state conferences. Similarly, the North American Council on Adoptable Children (NACAC; www.nacac.org) holds a yearly seminar for adoptive parents and people who are in the process of becoming adoptive parents.

POST-ADOPTION THERAPY

It is difficult for some adopted foster children to make the transition from foster child to adopted child. Perhaps your recently adopted child was helped by therapy throughout the foster placement and adoption process. But if this is not the case and your child seems to be struggling, you may want to investigate post-adoption therapy to provide your child with extra support.

RESPITE CARE

All parents (birth, foster, step, and adoptive) and other care providers (such as babysitters, day-care providers, and nannies) must be cool, calm, and collected when taking care of children with special needs. However, parents and care providers are only human and can become stressed out and emotionally drained from time to time. When this happens, they should seek respite care in order to refuel emotionally.

Respite care for adopted foster children with special needs should always be provided by trained, certified care providers who are patient and understanding with children who may act out while in their care. Ask your child's adoption worker or your fellow adoptive parents for their specific respite suggestions in your area.

Another way to locate local respite care providers for children with special needs is to visit the respite locator web page of the ARCH National Respite Network: chtop.org/ARCH/National-Respite-Locator.html.

KEY CHAPTER CONCEPTS

- Foster children may become available for adoption when both of their birth parents' parental rights have been terminated and there are no appropriate kinship placement options. Nearly 60 percent of children who are adopted from foster care are adopted by their foster parents.

- There are many benefits of adopting a child you have already been fostering. You are already familiar with the child's special needs, education plan, medical and family history, and behavioral issues.

- Permanent foster care can be an appropriate and viable permanency plan for foster children who are not available for adoption, but who also, for any number of reasons, cannot be reunited with their birth families.

- Steps for adopting a child from the foster care system include orientation, a home study, interviews, a background check, and pre-adoption training classes.

- Several financial assistance programs are available to adoptive parents of former foster children with special needs. These include the adoption subsidy and federal tax credits.

16

THE EXTENDED FOSTER CARE FAMILY

If you've detected a central theme in this book, it is that successful fostering comes down to teamwork, teamwork, and more teamwork. Think about fostering as a set of concentric circles. The innermost circle is the child's welfare team, also sometimes called the child's primary care team. This team is comprised of the child's caseworker, the child's foster parents, and, whenever appropriate, the child's birth parents.

The next circle of care providers consists of the child's health-care team: the pediatrician, dentist, therapist, and any other health-care providers or specialists helping to treat and maintain the child's health and well-being.

The third circle consists of the child's educational team: school administrators, the child's teachers, and anyone else involved in the implementation of the child's Individualized Education Program (IEP), including special-education teachers, guidance counselors, school psychologists, speech therapists, occupational therapists, and reading specialists.

The outermost circle is comprised of the foster parents' extended foster care team: formal and informal support networks; local, state, and national associations and support groups; and fellow foster parents and mentors. This chapter focuses on the extended foster care team.

TAPPING INTO YOUR FOSTER CARE SUPPORT NETWORK

It is important for new foster parents to seek support from a variety of sources, both formal and informal. A formal support group is one that is officially organized by a local, state, or national association, such as the National Foster Parent Association (NFPA). However, you can create an *informal* support group by simply deciding to meet once a month with some of your fostering friends for coffee and conversation about foster care.

To be a successful foster parent, it helps to be willing to reach out to your fellow foster parents for advice and encouragement. Having fostering in common can be an extraordinary bond. You might find that you and your fellow foster parents have other interests in common, too. Indeed, many lifelong friendships have begun in the positive environment of formal and informal foster parent support groups.

BENEFITS OF INFORMAL SUPPORT GROUPS

Official support groups and training sessions are helpful and informative, but sometimes there are no scheduled meetings when you need someone to talk to *right now*. If you have connected with fellow foster parents at a group meeting or training session, be sure to exchange contact information so that you can reach them by phone, text, or e-mail.

Even if you don't have anything pressing to discuss, there is something to be said for simply enjoying the company and camaraderie of other adults who share your deep interest in fostering. Your family and friends will try to help, but they may never fully understand the complexities of daily life with a foster child. Your fellow foster parents can empathize with you because of their firsthand experiences with the joys and challenges of fostering.

Think of your fellow foster parents, whether they are experienced foster parents or new to fostering like you, as your extended fostering family. The sense of togetherness and community can lift your spirits and give you the emotional sustenance you need to keep going.

222

It is particularly helpful to listen to experienced foster parents because they will never sugarcoat the challenges of fostering. At the same time, they will be the first to tell you how fulfilling it can be to help struggling children grow and develop.

Perhaps you already know some people who are fostering. If not, ask your caseworker to put you in touch with a fostering mentor. You will find that experienced foster parents are excellent teachers, eager to share their stories, knowledge, and practical tips.

BENEFITS OF FORMAL SUPPORT GROUPS

Attending formal support group meetings and training sessions is a great way to avoid burnout and to refuel emotionally. As John Donne famously wrote, "No man is an island, entire of itself." Indeed, all of us are members of the same human team, and formal support groups serve to remind us of this important fact.

When you first start going to support group meetings, you may feel overwhelmed or "underwhelmed" by what transpires. For instance, the conversation on a given evening might not flow well, or one particularly extroverted participant may dominate the group discussion in a way that you find annoying or less than helpful. However, even if you feel disappointed or ambivalent about your first few meetings, stick with the group for a while. Over time, as you adjust to the various personality styles of the participants, you will find yourself picking up helpful hints.

You may find that a fellow foster parent can put into words a particular emotion that you have felt about fostering but have never been able to express in a way that felt satisfying. Or perhaps another foster parent may describe a simple, practical solution to a problem you have been grappling with for a long time. These "aha!" moments certainly make attending formal support groups worthwhile. In addition, group members may share effective ways to destress or help you reprioritize certain issues in your life.

Even if most of your support group meetings revolve around specific training topics, there is usually a little bit of time before, after, and even during meetings to chat about other subjects. This is an excellent way to identify foster parents you click with and want to meet informally outside of these sessions. In addition, people who run support groups are a good source of information. Call them whenever you have a question about any aspect of fostering. They will be happy to send you pamphlets and other reading material about specific topics.

In sum, formal and informal support groups provide you with precious connections to other foster parents. Knowing that there are people out there who understand your profound desire to help children in need can be very comforting. Many foster parents say that the value of these connections to an extended foster care family cannot be overstated.

OFFICIAL SUPPORT NETWORKS

Official national, state, and local support networks are available to foster parents throughout the United States. They are sources of up-to-date information, as well as hubs that can link you to other helpful organizations.

THE NATIONAL FOSTER PARENT ASSOCIATION (NFPA)

The National Foster Parent Association (NFPA) is the only national organization that strives to support foster parents and remains a consistently strong voice on behalf of all children. The NFPA was born in 1972 out of a need for a nationwide support network and advocacy group for foster parents in the United States. It is a nonprofit, volunteer organization headquartered in Gig Harbor, Washington.

The NFPA has grown from an original group of 926 foster parents, 210 social workers, and 59 other professionals to an organization that represents thousands of foster families nationwide through foster parent affiliates. Each year, the NFPA sponsors numerous events and projects, including a national conference for the support and training of foster parents. Many new and experienced foster parents have benefited from attending this yearly conference and from participating in various other NFPA-sponsored events and activities.

A major purpose of NFPA is to draw together people, agencies, and professionals in a coordinated, working relationship. The primary goals of the NFPA are to …

- Promote the delivery of services and support to foster families.

- Support quality foster care by promoting excellence and best practices.

- Provide services and support to state and local foster parent associations.

- Develop and provide education and training and disseminate information to the public.

- Advocate at the local, state, and national levels, and promote networking and collaboration.

- Promote a positive image of family foster care, create greater visibility, and encourage active involvement in child welfare.

Membership in the NFPA is open to anyone interested in improving the foster care system and enhancing the lives of children and families. The membership application is available online. Affiliate memberships are open to local or state foster parent associations, local or state agencies, social workers, foster parents, and all other individuals interested in the foster care program.

YOUR STATE AND LOCAL ASSOCIATIONS

Each of the 50 states has its own foster parent association. For information regarding your state foster parent association, go the NFPA website and click on the link that says "State Organizations." There you will find information for your state foster parent association, as well as county and local foster parent associations and support groups.

Communicating with and learning from your state and local organizations is an essential part of information-gathering for all potential foster parents. This is because many specifics of fostering—such as requirements for becoming a foster parent and monthly reimbursement stipends—vary from state to state.

YOU'LL NEVER WALK ALONE

If you are considering becoming a foster parent, you will likely have questions, concerns, and even doubts along with your sense of happy anticipation. That's natural and normal. Remember, it is never too soon to reach out to those who are already involved in the foster care system. These individuals will welcome your inquiries. It's not an imposition! They are eager to share their knowledge and their stories.

As you walk down the path of foster parenting, one thing is for certain: you will never need to walk alone. Here's wishing you the best of luck on your journey.

KEY CHAPTER CONCEPTS

- The extended foster care team includes formal and informal support groups.

- Both formal and informal support groups are key sources of encouragement and emotional sustenance. In both formal and informal support groups, participants share useful information and solutions to problems.

- Your extended foster care family will understand what you are going through better than anyone else. Your extended foster care family will offer emotional support and renewal and a sense of shared purpose, fellowship, and community.

- Experienced foster parents and mentors are more than willing to share their knowledge and practical tips with potential and new foster parents.

- Official support networks, such as the National Foster Parent Association (NFPA) and state and local foster parent associations, provide foster parents with an abundance of tools, resources, training, encouragement, and support.

A

RECOMMENDED READING

Bridge, Andrew. *Hope's Boy: A Memoir*. New York: Hyperion, 2008.

Cameron, Theresa. *Foster Care Odyssey: A Black Girl's Story*. Jackson, MS: University Press of Mississippi, 2002.

Comer, James P., and Alvin F. Poussaint. *Raising Black Children: Two Leading Psychiatrists Confront the Educational, Social, and Emotional Problems Facing Black Children*. New York: Plume, 1992.

Funk, David. *Love & Logic: Solutions for Kids with Special Needs*. Golden, CO: Love and Logic Press, 2002.

Gray, Deborah D. *Attaching in Adoption: Practical Tools for Today's Parents*. Indianapolis: Perspectives Press, 2002.

Harrison, Kathy. *Another Place at the Table*. New York: Tarcher, 2003.

———. *One Small Boat: The Story of a Little Girl, Lost Then Found*. New York: Tarcher, 2006.

Holmes, Margaret M., and Sasha J. Mudlaff. *A Terrible Thing Happened: A Story for Children Who Have Witnessed Violence or Trauma*. Washington, D.C.: Magination Press, 2000.

Hughes, Daniel A. *Building the Bonds of Attachment: Awakening Love in Deeply Troubled Children*. Lanham, MD: Jason Aronson Publishers, Inc., 2006.

Keck, Gregory C., and Regina M. Kupecky. *Parenting the Hurt Child: Helping Adoptive Families Heal and Grow*. Colorado Springs, CO: Piñon Press, 2002.

Krebs, Betsy, and Paul Pitcoff. *Beyond the Foster Care System: The Future for Teens*. Piscataway, NJ: Rutgers University Press, 2006.

Rowell, Victoria. *The Women Who Raised Me: A Memoir*. New York: William Morrow, 2007.

Schooler, Jayne. *What Parents Need to Know When Siblings Are Separated*. Westport, CT: Bergin & Garvey, 2002.

Shirk, Martha. *On Their Own: What Happens to Kids When They Age Out of the Foster Care System*. New York: Basic Books, 2006.

Stoller, John L. *Parenting Other People's Children: Understanding and Repairing Reactive Attachment Disorder*. New York: Vantage Press, 2006.

Temple-Plotz, Lana, Ted P. Stricklett, Christena B. Baker, and Michael N. Sterba. *Practical Tools for Foster Parents*. Boystown, NE: Boys Town Press, 2002.

WORKS CITED OR CONSULTED

American Public Human Services Association. "Medicaid Access for Youth Aging Out of Foster Care." 2007. www.aphsa.org/Home/Doc/Medicaid-Access-for-Youth-Aging-Out-of-Foster-Care-Rpt.pdf.

Blomquist, Geraldine M., and Paul B. Blomquist. *Zachary's New Home: A Story for Foster and Adopted Children*. New York: Magination Press, 1990.

Briguglio, Bethany. "Foster Mother's Dedication Earns Children's Appreciation and an Award." *The Community Advocate* (Westborough, MA), May 11, 2007.

Magazines

Chasnoff, Ira J. *The Nature of Nurture: Biology, Environment, and the Drug-Exposed Child.* Chicago: National Training Institute, 2001.

Craft, Carrie. "Developmental Grieving." About.com. adoption. about.com/cs/legalissues/a/Holiday_strugl.htm.

Craft, Carrie. "Foster Children and Your Extended Family During the Holidays." About.com. adoption.about.com/od/fostering/a/ fosterholiday.htm.

Craft, Carrie. "How to Create a Safety Plan." About.com. adoption. about.com/od/parenting/a/howtosafety.htm.

DePanfilis, Diane, and Clara Daining. Hitting the M.A.R.C.: Establishing Foster Care Minimum Adequate Rates for Children. New York: Children's Rights, National Foster Parent Association, and the University of Maryland School of Social Work, October 2007. www.childrensrights.org/ policy-projects/foster-care/hitting-the-marc-foster-care- reimbursement-rates/.

Edelstein, Susan. "When Foster Children Leave: Helping Foster Parents to Grieve." *Child Welfare* 60.7 (1981): 467–73.

Federal Reserve Bank of Atlanta (unattributed article). "Transitioning Youth from Foster Care to Successful Adulthood," *Partners in Community and Economic Development* 17.2 (2007). www.frbatlanta.org/invoke.cfm?objectid=141D317E-5056- 9F12-12C8293B081CD754&method=display_body.

Foster, Donna Gillespie. "The Voice of a Child." *Fostering Perspectives* 4.2 (2000). ssw.unc.edu/fcrp/fp/fp_vol4no2/voice_of_a_child. htm.

Graham, Jennifer M. "Ken-Crest Cares for Medically Fragile Children." *The Lutheran,* February 2003. findarticles.com/p/ articles/mi_qa3942/is_200302/ai_n9235056/print.

Hale-Benson, Janice E. *Black Children: Their Roots, Culture, and Learning Styles*. Baltimore: Johns Hopkins University Press, 1986.

Heidbuurt, Judith. "All in the Family Home: The Biological Children of Parents Who Foster," a conference presentation delivered in July 2004 at the 18th Annual Conference on Treatment Foster Care. www.ffta.org/research_outcomes/abstracts18_heidbuurt.pdf.

Helfer, Ray E., and C. Henry Kempe. *The Battered Child*. 3d ed., rev. and expanded. Chicago: University of Chicago Press, 1980.

Hopson, Darlene. *Different and Wonderful: Raising Black Children in a Race-Conscious Society*. New York: Fireside Books, 1992.

Killian, Kelly L. *The Adoption.com Guide to Foster Adoption*. E-book: foster-child.adoption.com/parents/foster-adoption-ebook.html.

Kiser, Kim. "Fostering Healthy Brains." *Minnesota Medicine* Minnesota Medical Association, March 2006. www.minnesotamedicine.com/PastIssues/March2006/PulseBrainMarch2006/tabid/2356/Default.aspx.

Kitze, Carrie A., and Rob Williams. *I Don't Have Your Eyes*. Warren, NJ: EMK Press, 2003.

Lambert, Bruce. "Ray Helfer, Leader in Preventing Abuse of Children, Is Dead at 62." *New York Times*, February 10, 1992. http://query.nytimes.com/gst/fullpage.html?res=9E0CE7DD133BF933A25751C0A964958260&scp=1&sq=ray+helfer&st=nyt.

Mallon, Gerald P., and Peg McCartt Hess. *Child Welfare for the 21st Century*. New York: Columbia University Press, 2005.

McBride, Rebecca. *Handbook for Youth in Foster Care*, New York: Office of Children and Family Services. January 2007. www.ocfs.state.ny.us/main/publications/Pub5028.pdf.

McCrone, John. "Rebels with a Cause." *New Scientist News Service*. January 2000. Reed Business Information: Sutton, UK. www.newscientist.com/channel/being-human/teenagers/mg16522224.200.

McMahon, John, ed. "When I Become a Foster Parent ...." *Fostering Perspectives* 10.1 (2005). ssw.unc.edu/fcrp/fp/fp_v10n1/when.htm.

National Resource Center for Family-Centered Practice and Permanency Planning at the Hunter College School of Social Work. "Policies on Placing Siblings in Out of Home Care (Last Updated December 28, 2005)." www.hunter.cuny.edu/socwork/nrcfcpp/downloads/policy-issues/Sibling_Placement_Policies.pdf.

New York State Office of Children and Family Services. *Keeping Siblings Connected: A White Paper on Siblings in Foster Care and Adoptive Placements in New York State*. June 2007. www.ocfs.state.ny.us/main/reports/sibling%20white%20paper%20wes.pdf.

———. and the Center for the Development of Human Services. *The Child Development Guide*. 2002. www.bsc-cdhs.org/fosterparenttraining/pdfs/ChildDevelGuide.pdf.

Phillips, Christopher. "Foster-Care System Struggles to Keep Siblings Living Together." *APAOnline* 29.1 (1998). www.apa.org/monitor/jan98/sibs.html.

Prevent Child Abuse America. *Preparing to Be A Foster Parent*. Chicago: Prevent Child Abuse America, 2001.

Scheppler, Vincenette. *Professional Parenthood: A Guide for Foster Care*. Arlington, TX: Arvin Publications. www.arvinpublications.com/parenthood.html.

St. Clair, Brita. *99 Ways to Drive Your Child Sane*. Glenwood Springs, CO: Families by Design, 1999.

Thomas, Nancy L. *When Love Is Not Enough: A Guide to Parenting Children with Reactive Attachment Disorder*. Glenwood Springs, CO: Families by Design, 1997.

Unattributed article. "Separation, Loss, and Foster Parent Retention," *Children's Services Practice Notes* 12.4 (1997). ssw.unc.edu/fcrp/cspn/vol2_no4/separation_loss_and_foster_parent_retention.htm.

Unattributed article. "Suggestions for Engaging Birth Parents." *Fostering Perspectives* 4.2 (2000). ssw.unc.edu/fcrp/fp/fp_vol4no2/suggestions_engaging.htm.

Unattributed article. "Understanding Birth Family Grief," Fostering Perspectives 4.2 (2000). ssw.unc.edu/fcrp/fp/fp_vol4no2/understanding_birth_family_grief.htm.

Vera Institute of Justice. *Foster Children: How You Can Create a Positive Educational Experience for the Foster Child*. New York: Vera Institute of Justice, 2004. www.vera.org/publication_pdf/241_452.pdf.

Wen, Patricia. "Choices of the Heart: An Adoptive Mother Has Second Thoughts," *The Boston Sunday Globe*, September 23, 2007. www.boston.com/news/local/articles/2007/09/23/choices_of_the_heart/.

B

KEY ORGANIZATIONS

The National Foster Parent Association (NFPA)
7512 Stanich Lane, Suite 6
Gig Harbor, WA 98335
Phone: 1-800-557-5238
Fax: 253-853-4001
E-mail: info@NFPAonline.org
www.nfpaonline.org

For information regarding your state foster parent association, visit the main NFPA website, and from there, click on "State Organizations" (www.nfpaonline.org/reploc/). You will find a map of the United States, including Alaska and Hawaii. Click on your state for the name of and contact information for your state foster parent association, as well as county and local foster parent associations and support groups in your state.

The NFPA website also provides links to organizations and websites of general interest to foster parents: www.nfpaonline.org/content/?page=LINKS&nmenu=4&title=Foster%20Parent%20Links.

Adoptive Families Magazine
Editorial and Advertising Offices
39 West 37th Street, 15th Floor
New York, NY 10018
Phone: 646-366-0830
Fax: 646-366-0842
E-mail: letters@adoptivefamilies.com
www.adoptivefamilies.com

The Attachment Institute of New England
21 Cedar Street
Worcester, MA 01609
Phone: 508-799-2663 (BOND)
Fax: 508-753-9779
www.attachmentnewengland.com

CaringBridge
1995 Rahn Cliff Court, Suite 200
Eagan, MN 55122
Phone: 651-452-7940
Fax: 651-681-7115
caringbridge.org

Casey Family Programs
1300 Dexter Avenue North, 3rd Floor
Seattle, WA 98109
Phone: 206-282-7300
Fax: 206-282-3555
www.casey.org/Home

Child Welfare Information Gateway
Children's Bureau/ACYF
1250 Maryland Avenue, SW, 8th Floor
Washington, D.C. 20024
Phone: 703-385-7565 or 1-800-394-3366
E-mail: info@childwelfare.gov
www.childwelfare.gov

Institute for Human Services (I.H.S.)
North American Resource Center for Child Welfare
Gwinn House
1706 East Broad Street
Columbus, OH 43203
Phone: 614-251-6000
Fax: 614-251-6005
www.ihs-trainet.com

Jim Casey Youth Opportunities Initiative
222 South Central, Suite 305
St. Louis, MO 63105
Phone: 314-863-7000
Fax: 314-863-7003
www.jimcaseyyouth.org

John H. Chafee Foster Care Independence Program
Administration for Children and Families
370 L'Enfant Promenade, SW
Washington, D.C. 20447
www.acf.hhs.gov/programs/cb/programs_fund/state_tribal/jh_chafee.htm

Neighbor to Family
Corporate Offices
Brown & Brown Building
220 South Ridgewood Avenue, Suite 260
Daytona Beach, FL 32114
Phone: 386-523-1440
Fax: 386-523-1459
www.neighbortofamily.org

North American Council on Adoptable Children (NACAC)
970 Raymond Avenue, Suite 106
St. Paul, MN 55114
Phone: 651-644-3036
Fax: 651-644-9848
E-mail: info@nacac.org
www.nacac.org

Prevent Child Abuse America (PCA)
National Office
500 North Michigan Avenue, Suite 200
Chicago, IL 60611
Phone: 312-663-3520
Fax: 312-939-8962
E-mail: mailbox@preventchildabuse.org
Information and Referral: 1-800-CHILDREN (1-800-244-5373)
www.preventchildabuse.org

INDEX

F

Social Security benefits, 216

states, 215

tax credits, 215

WIC program, 216

covered expenses, 59

education, 60

exceptional circumstances, 58

federal/state funding

exceptional circumstances, 58

IV-E, 56

reimbursement payments, 57-58

Social Security Act, 56

noncovered expenses, 60

receiving reimbursement payments, 61

requirements, 40

sibling groups, 135

finding support, 41, 222

fire safety, 182

first placements, 63

agency support, 73-75

choices, 64

example success story, 66

home preparations, 72-73

preparations for existing family, 68

adjustments, 69

appropriate versus inappropriate touch, 71

biological children as role models, 69

nurturing communication, 70

treating all children fairly, 70

preplacement meetings, 67

process, 66

formal support groups, 223

Foster Child Bill of Rights, 36

foster children

choosing, 40

defined, 1

foster parents

criteria, 3

defined, 2

legal requirements, 3

responsibilities, 4

behavior management, 5

biological parent communication, 6

easing separation pains, 5

Foster Parents' Rights and Responsibilities, 36

"Foster-care system struggles to keep siblings living together," 134

FosterClub.com, 52

future placements, 203

G

Q

R

S

T